The Year of the Woman

A Guide for Turning Sadness into Strength

Written by Ikeshia Capre

www.ikeshiacapre.com
Cover Design by Nnenna-Lovette Design, Graphics and Web Design Services
Edited by Val Pugh-Love
ISBN 978-0-9966247-1-8
Photographed by Mindy Dowdle

To purchase books, visit
www.ikeshiacapre.com
Follow me on social media:
Instagram: Ikeshia Capre

Other businesses owned and operated
by Ikeshia Capre:

Facebook: Power of Pink Hair Collections
Instagram: p.o.p_collections
Twitter: popcollections1
www.popcollections.com

To all those I love...

     I can't put into words how much I care about those who believed in me while I was completing this project. It means the world to me that I have such a strong support system, given the circumstances were quite different a few years ago. I can truly say this would not have been possible without you all, and I will be forever grateful. I want to continue to make you proud, and I want to share my passion for writing as much as and as often as I can. I want to be great; however, I know I will never be great without you all. I believe there is no limit to what a person can do, especially with the right people around them. I can genuinely say I am blessed with the right people in my life. If I haven't said it enough, I want the opportunity to express it now. Thank you.

                   -Ikeshia Capre

Section 1:

"Not everyone will appreciate your good heart.
Some will accept your kindness and disrespect you in return."

-Tony Gaskins

Dear Broken Heart,

I know it hurts. You've tried to tell many people just how deep you were cut, but no one was listening. Dammit! They said everything would be okay! They said you would find love again. They said time would heal all wounds. They even said be glad it happened now rather than later. WHAT THE FUCK? You didn't want this to happen at all. Besides, how would they know what would happen? I mean, let's be honest... Finding a man when you're a black woman closer to your thirties is hard. For many years, you hid behind your educational success, your friendships, and your jobs. No one could have you. At least, not a man anyway. When the opportunity came to give yourself up to experience what you thought at the time was "true love" and to feel like a real woman, you hit the ground running fast. It was too fast for your liking, but you went along for the ride because his eyes lit up when he saw you.

What was happening to you? You were beginning to get soft! You started putting his happiness before your own. No one came before you. EVER! However, you were ready to love. Ready to be open. Ready to give it your all. But, somewhere along the way, things got hard. Things got tough. Your smile turned into tears. Your joy turned into hurt. Your happiness turned into hate. It was like watching the main character of your favorite movie die right in front of you...except you were the main character. You looked around waiting for someone to tell you this was all a dream. You grabbed your chest trying to find the air to breathe because the life had just gotten sucked out of you. That wasn't happening to you! I mean, how the fuck could someone who swore by their heart, pretend they love you and tell you that you were God-sent? Apparently, he was a bullshitter!

Unfortunately, you didn't see his bullshittin' ass coming. Maybe, you refused to see it because you were forced to open up. You were already vulnerable. Already all in. Let's face it; you fell flat on your face. That was it. That was the end. No more happiness. No more joy. No more love. How are you going to move on with your life? Who is going to pick up the fucking shattered pieces lying all around you? You don't have a clue nor a logical guess. You can't even phone a friend because there are no words left. There's nothing left. You gave it all you had, and now you're empty. Empty soul. Empty heart. Empty mind. What now?

***

It was 8:38 a.m. on April 27, 2015. I woke up to my phone buzzing like crazy on my marble nightstand next to my bed. Where I lived at the time, there was hardly any cell phone reception. So, good luck if you wanted to talk to me on the phone. As I rolled out of bed with my eyes barely open, I answered the phone right before it stopped ringing.

I answered groggily, "*Hello?*"

With evident irritation in his voice, he said, "*I've called you three times. Why didn't you answer me?!*"

"My phone didn't ring. I'm sorry!"

He knew the reception in my apartment was janky. Why was he on my case? It was too early for this shit. I didn't have to be at work until noon, and this motherfucker was interrupting my sleep. Plus, our 8:30 a.m. phone call was a ritual. He had nothing new to tell me except that he was on his way to work, he would call me when he got off, and that he loves me. Nothing new. It wasn't that I was bored with our conversations we had every morning. I looked forward to them, but I was completely caught off guard by his attitude that I didn't answer this one time. The only time we've never talked was once while he was overseas. ONCE IN NINE MONTHS! So, the attitude was a bit dramatic in my mind. After I got done pleading my case about my janky ass reception, the next couple sentences out of his mouth were going to change my life forever.

"Well, I just wanted to talk to you. This is becoming tough. I'm getting overwhelmed and stressed out. I can't seem to talk to you at all. All you ever do is talk about the wedding and school. Like I can't... I... just... don't know if I want this relationship anymore."

You know how the music plays in the background of the movie and then suddenly stops because something dramatic is getting ready to happen? Yeah, that was me right after those words slipped from his tongue. As my eyes got bigger, my heart started beating fast, and my throat began to close. I knew in my heart this was it. I jumped out of my bed that had double mattresses on it and walked slowly to the living room. I curled my feet under my ass and sat before I responded.

"What do you mean you don't want this relationship anymore? I sent our save-the-dates out yesterday! I talk about the wedding all the time because we are getting married in less than six months, and you're not here to plan it with me. I talk about school because we're both in our master's programs."

After he calmed himself, he replied, *"I know. I'm just stressed and overwhelmed."*

My voice began to shake. "This isn't supposed to stress you. If anything, I'm supposed to be the person you call when you are feeling stressed and overwhelmed."

Silence…

When I finally pulled myself together and organized the little bit of thought process I had left, I offered to return all his Christmas gifts, including the ring.

With surprise, he began, *"You don't want to talk about this when I get off?"*

As much as I wanted to talk about things, I went from immediately being upset to just fucking anger. I mean, the whole idea of us getting married was his. He just played the fuck out of me, and I was just supposed to take it? Nah. Not on my watch!

With an attitude, I replied, "Nope."

We hung up the phone, and my eyes started to fill with tears. I called my job and told them I needed to take a personal day. My head began to hurt because I had been crying so hard. As I tried to wipe my eyes, I began sending out text messages to all my close friends: *"We called off the wedding."* I was hurt. It was the most hurt I've ever been. I didn't know how I was going to tell my family, my coworkers, and believe or not, Facebook. I am very private when it comes to my relationships, but I assumed because we were engaged I was safe to disclose the man I would be fucking for the next forty years. Clearly, I was wrong. I knew I wasn't going to post a status like most do when they go through a breakup, but I know people aren't stupid. Going from posting Christmas and engagement photos to none is an obvious clue I couldn't cover up. Fuck social media!

As I continued to cry, it became harder to breathe because my nose was becoming stuffed. I balled up some toilet paper as I blew my nose, and then I fell back on the couch and stared at his birthday gifts that I planned to send him. He was turning thirty-three in six days, but I felt like this was a horrible teenage love. I took off my 4-carat ring and placed it in a yellow envelope. Along with the ring was a workout book - he was into fitness - and a heart-shaped picture frame I had painted with my picture inside. Half of the frame was painted black, and the other half was painted red with white letters that read: *"I love you."* In addition, I stuffed three more wallet-sized photos in a birthday card to add to his picture collection of me because I knew he was out there all alone, so I thought. I thought the pictures would change his mind or have him reminisce about all the moments we shared. It was a good attempt, I thought.

I continued to cry off and on all day. Speaking to my best friend throughout the day via text, he told me everything was going to be okay, and I would get through it. He was always so positive and wanted the best for me. He didn't like the idea of me getting married anyway. But, as a good friend, he supported me through the decision. I'm sure it was hard for him to see me go down a path he knew wasn't meant for me. He wanted the best for me, as I did for him. It's not every day that you find friends like that.

Nevertheless, I didn't think I could get through this hard time. Actually, I knew I couldn't. I couldn't believe this was happening to me. I spent money on a wedding dress, my friends spent money on bridesmaids' dresses, and I put the deposit down on the venue. All my friends knew that my money is important to me. When I feel someone is trying to screw me over, all hell breaks loose! This time, breaking loose wasn't an option because he was states away, and I knew his family would side with him before siding with me. Translation: I wasn't going to see a dime of that money. *FUCK!*

7:30 p.m. rolled around, and I hadn't turned on any lights in my apartment. I sat in the dark all day and night. I didn't want to see myself walking around in my own house because I felt so disgusted. I was scared that if I saw my reflection on anything, there would be puffy red eyes and a woman who was broken inside. I just couldn't do it. I had never felt so helpless. I had never felt like I had failed miserably at something since my junior high school track meet when I false started for the 300-meters hurdle race. I let my team down, my school down, and myself down. It was the most embarrassing moment of my life. I didn't think anything could be worse than that, but I was wrong.

I mustered up the courage to open my phone and select my ex-mother-in-law's name to tell her she was not going to carry that title. When I hit send, my phone rang within in a matter of two minutes. As we talked, I thanked her for allowing me to be a part of her family.

Her final words were, *"Take care of yourself. Heal your soul."*

At the time, the words *heal your soul* went in one ear and out the other. I felt so numb. I just wanted to hide in my apartment and pray the reception would never be restored so my connection to the world would be forever cut off. This was too much.

I shipped his birthday gifts with the engagement ring included. Three days after his birthday, I received a message. He wanted to talk. There was no apology included, so I chose to be a hard-ass and made him wait until I was finished with school that weekend before we talked. I didn't want to seem desperate to get back with him. In fact, I had refused to be desperate since I wasn't the one who started this fuckery in the first place. After giving him the timeframe I was available to talk, there was no reply. In fact, there was no reply all weekend. Talk about a backfire in my face. It bothered me that the man that told me I was God-sent a year ago now acts as though he doesn't want to talk - after initiating the conversation. What a dick!

After putting my ego to the side, I realized if I wanted to work things out, I had to show him I was willing to work and fight for the relationship. I had never fought for any relationship. After a weekend of waiting and waiting, finally on Mother's Day, I sent a message saying I was home from school and available if we were going to talk. He finally responded saying he would call after his group dinner. I was taken aback by the "group dinner" comment because he doesn't socialize with his coworkers. He always told me, there was no point in making new friends because he would only be stationed at his base until his master's degree was complete, which was in June. At the time, June was less than thirty days away. Maybe they were saying their final goodbyes, I thought. Maybe it was bullshit. I didn't know what to think.

When 8:30 p.m. rolled around, my phone laid dead. The longer I sat Indian-style by my bedroom window with my phone propped up on the window sill to receive some inkling of service, the more I realized this was it. The time had come for me to give up. I took a deep breath with my eyes filled with tears and began to type the message I'd never thought I would have written a year prior. *"I don't know what happened today. We were supposed to talk, but it appears you do not care. Bottom line, I wasn't ready to have a child, and I don't believe that attempting to make someone have a child is okay. I hope you get the help you need. Good luck. God Bless. "*

It made me sick to think I would have married someone who tried to force me to have a child to ensure commitment. Nevertheless, I stuck with it hoping I could convince him having a child wasn't going to make a relationship better. But indeed, rip it apart. I was ringless and manless as I thought *"What the hell am I going to tell my mom? "* It didn't matter what I told her. She had followed my father around for almost thirty years after he had other children and married twice - both times to other women. I wasn't going to do that. I wasn't going to be the woman who desperately needed a man so badly that I was willing to do anything to have him. I didn't want my mom to know her baby girl was hurt. She's never seen me hurt about a guy since the time I lost my virginity at age fourteen.

When most people become hurt after a breakup, they pour their heart out on social media which then sparks the questions from family and friends: *What happened? Are you okay?* I, for one, kept my family out of my relationships both on and off social media, but I took a chance on this one. Getting the family involved was a big step for me. Once I knew we were getting engaged, I let him meet my mother. Wrong move. Eventually, I had to tell her the wedding was off. She paid for a dress that she will now never wear. Again, *FUCK!*

A few weeks later, I sent a message to his mother asking if her shitty ass son could give me my money back for the bridesmaids' dresses and deposit for the venue. I knew he had the money. He wasn't broke. Sixteen hundred dollars was nothing since he had been deployed for almost a year prior. His savings account was LIT. If he had a decent heart, he would've just given me the money back for involving my family and friends. I wasn't worried about my wedding dress. That cost I was willing to swallow, but shitting on my family and friends was a NO-NO! A few minutes later, she called me.

"Keshia, he said he got the gifts."

"Ok, well did he get the ring? I put it in the envelope, too!"

With surprise in her voice, she responded, *"Oh...well he never mentioned that."*

I thought to myself, *of course, he didn't mention that. There's a lot that motherfucker didn't mention.*

"Ok, well do you still have the tracking number for the gifts you sent?" she asked.

Again, I think to myself, *what the flying fuck does the tracking number have to do with anything? He has the gifts. The ring was included.*

Calmly, I responded, "No, I ended up throwing the receipt out. As a matter of fact, tell him to call me. We don't need to involve you. Tell him to man up and call me."

"Ok, I will get on the phone now and tell him to call you."

The phone hung up. Ten minutes later, I received a text: *I got the gifts. Thank you. There was no ring in the envelope. I didn't see it with the other gifts.*

Unfortunately, I was at work at the time, so calling him to cuss his ass out after receiving that message was not an option. I began to backtrack and think, *"Could the ring really have fallen out the bottom? No, it couldn't have! It had extra protection with bubble wrap inside the envelope, so I know it couldn't have just fallen out! He's lying! I know he is!*

After coming back to my senses, I replied. *"Well, I put the ring inside the envelope. Either you threw it away because you forgot it was in the package, or it fell out, and you lost it when you opened the package. Either way, I returned the ring."* While I had his attention, I needed to get more things off my chest, *"You need to man up and stop hiding behind your mother. You shouldn't be relaying messages through her."*

And, as a smart ass like he is, this motherfucker had the nerve to say, *"Are you mad or nah?"*

For a grown ass man to respond in that manner, I thought this was the worst decision I could have made. Not only was he petty as fuck, but he was also having his mother fight his battle. On top of that, he was lying about not receiving the ring and responded as if I wasn't shit. He showed his true colors, and I had to admit, I thank God all this happened before I said, *"I do."*

Before I knew it, I snapped back, *"Nah, I'm not mad. I'm glad I dodged the bullet."*

As his final response, he said, *"Well, thank you anyway for all the good and the bad things you gave me."*

That last response threw me over the edge; I had to get one thing set straight and clear. His remark thanking me for the bad things was a low blow and cut me deep. As previously described at the end of my first book, I discussed one of the hardest things I've ever had to discuss in my life. The person who I was going to marry gave me an STD. Yes, you read that correctly - an STD. Once

I received the news from the doctor, I frantically started researching the causes, effects, and cures. What I found was that it was not curable and had lifelong effects physically and emotionally. Not only that, I wasn't able to determine who had given me the STD.

That was a hard pill for me to swallow when I first found out I had this STD. I'd thought to myself, "My hoeing days caught up with me!" When I broke the news to him, I blamed myself. Even though ninety-five percent of the time I practiced safe sex, something must have crept through that five percent window. At the time, because I was so upset balling my eyes out, I told him he didn't have to stay with me, but he insisted he would. Not only did he stay, but he never gave any reaction to me telling him the news. Instead, he openly admitted to sleeping with many women and seemed okay with the news.

HELLO!!! CAN WE SAY RED FUCKING FLAG!

In addition to that, I thought back to us talking over the phone while he was overseas. He mentioned to me how his buddy found out his girlfriend had the same STD I had, and she gave it to his buddy. At the time, I cringed because I knew that had to be devastating news. As the conversation went on, with hesitation, he asked me, *"Would you be with me if I had an STD?"* Now, I've dated a lot. I mean a lot. And, in the thirty years I've been living or at least the sixteen years I've been sexually active, not one male I've ever encountered asked me that question.

At the time, I assumed he was only asking to see if I would love him through thick and thin since we were discussing marriage, but he never confessed to having an STD. For whatever reason, I wasn't thinking he was having sex with anyone nor did I think I had anything to worry about in the future. We had never been intimate because he was overseas, so anticipating an STD on our first encounter would have never crossed my mind. Now, I knew damn well I wasn't going to be with anyone who had an STD, especially one that didn't have a cure. However, I wanted to see what he had to say. Of course, he never really answered. Instead, he quickly laughed it off as if the question was not a big deal.

As I rode home that night after work, I just couldn't believe how ignorant this dude was and how stupid I had been for wasting my time. I knew from the beginning this was a bad move, but I kept moving forward. I didn't know if it was because I thought I would never find anyone, or if I was truly at a place in my life where I deserved true love. One thing I did know was that I was not ever speaking to that fuck face again. Most importantly, I was thankful that we did not live in the same state because I might have gone postal on his ass.

A month later, I arrived at my old boss's home, and we began to catch up on what had been going on since the breakup. She asked me had he contacted me, and I said no. I didn't want to let her know I was hurt, so I played hard and began to act like I didn't care to speak to or hear from him again. Unfortunately, the next line out of her mouth literally sucked the life out of me.

"Good!! Because he's already with someone else! You don't need him!"

Barely getting the words out of my mouth, I replied, "Oh really?!"

"Yeah, I guess. He uploaded a picture of him and another black girl on his social media, and people think that's his new girlfriend."

That moment, I thought to myself, *it hasn't even been thirty days since I talked to this fool! How in hell does he have a new girlfriend that quick? He just graduated from school and moved to his next base! This is not possible!* Little did I know, it was very fucking possible. I swear I didn't care about him anymore, but I had to know! I had to see who she was! I needed to see who she was, or even if this was true. Maybe, this was just a woman who he became friends with before he left the base. I mean, I did know about one black woman who attended a group dinner, but she didn't seem like his type.

At this point, I had unfriended him from all social media because I wanted no parts of seeing his ass. But to my mistake, I never blocked him which gave me the access to search his name. I was not able to see anything that stood out on his timeline, but I had access to his friend list. As I scrolled through, I tried to see women who appeared to be new friends on his list. I had no luck until I came to one woman who stood out. She had deep dark chocolate skin. Her teeth were pearly white and lined up perfectly. Her home state was the state he was in when finishing his master's degree.

I clicked on her profile, and surprisingly, it was public. I scrolled through her timeline and right before I closed out, I came across a picture of both her and him… and a little girl. I blinked my eyes rapidly because I wasn't trying to cry in front of my old boss. I didn't want to let her know what

I found. As I kept scrolling down her timeline, I came across her profile picture that was of him and her. I knew she was the one my boss had mentioned. I looked at the date of the picture and immediately got sick because it was dated during the time he and I were still engaged. If I could have passed out, I would have.

I sat there looking at the profile picture with disgust because she was wearing his hoodie I had in the month prior when I visited him. I could not believe my eyes. I could not believe he had been cheating on me. Quickly, I got up and told my boss I had to go home. Then, I drove to my apartment like a bat out of hell. I screenshot the picture of him and her and sent it to his mother. I told his mother that her son lied about not getting the ring and that he'd been seeing this girl while we were engaged. I assumed he gave her the ring because her profile read that she was engaged. My fingers were moving a mile a minute. My heart was beating fast, and I was shaking because I was so worked up. I even took it upon myself to text him and tell him how much of a coward he was for being with another woman while we were engaged. I got no response back. Go figure. His mother, on the other hand, did respond.

"Yes, he did come home with her and stayed here for about four days, but I kicked them out. I do not like her because she is a liar. He, his sister, and I got into a big fight, and I told him that girl is not welcomed back into my home. I don't know what his problem is, but after I told him to leave, I have not heard from him since then. And, I have no clue where he is currently located."

As I read the text, I couldn't hold the tears back anymore. Not only did this *motherfucker* try to pressure me to conceive a child, but I also got an STD (which I believe came from him), and was cheated on while we were engaged. I had had enough. I was officially broken. What the fuck do I do now? All this time I never knew the reason for us breaking up, but now I know. How was I going to explain to my family and friends that the guy I thought I was going to marry was with another woman? Just fucking how?

Mission 1: Camp Counselors

First thing's first. I went to the gas station and purchased more cigarettes. I had never smoked a day in my life until the day we had officially broken up. I remember I had on white and black sheer pants that could be worn on a beach and a black tank top. Unfortunately, everything in my life was the opposite of the beach. Shit, I was experiencing a tornado at that moment, and I didn't know when it was going to end. As I got my cigarettes, I looked through my phone and texted an old fling. I told him I wanted to see him that night. Not tomorrow night. Not next week. I wanted to see him as soon as he punched out on his time card.

He responded, *"I work 'til 1 a.m."* I didn't care. I just didn't want to sit at home and cry. I had done enough of that over the past two and a half months, and I was determined to pull it together. I needed to get revenge. Go back to my old ways. At least for a night. I needed to feel like I didn't care anymore. I needed to feel like I wasn't fazed. I needed to feel like I didn't get played.

As I pulled up at my old fling's job, I lit my cigarette and sat patiently until 1:00 a.m. As I sat, I thought back to a year prior when he confessed to me that he was a father and could still possibly be with the mother of his child. However, none of that mattered that night. I didn't care who he was involved with currently or if he was interested in someone else. I just knew I had to get my mind off my current situation.

When he walked up to my car, with confusion, he asked, *"When did you start smoking cigarettes?"*

"Um, about two months ago. Some things happened, and I've been having a difficult time dealing with it. So, this is what I'm doing."

"You don't need to be smoking. I've never known you to do anything like that. You've always been a good girl. Don't be smoking cigarettes!"

"Well, right now this is what I want to do. I'm not going to do it too much longer. I kind of don't know what I'm doing anyway."

"Well, I'm almost off work. Do you want to come back to my place and chill for a second?"

"Yeah, sure."

As I waited for him to get off work, I kept wondering how I got here. How did I go from being engaged and feeling on top of the world to being another woman scorned? None of it made sense to me at the time. My mind was all over the place. When he clocked out, I followed him back to his studio apartment. He told me a lot of his belongings were taken to his sister's house because his apartment building was infested with bedbugs. (FUCK!) I was instantly turned off. I knew that I wanted to get my mind off things, but the idea of me lying on my back and a bug crawling on me wasn't going down.

He eventually sent a message to his buddy and then quickly turned to me and asked if I wanted to smoke weed. I knew that would get my mind off things, but I wasn't willing to risk losing my job. After all, I needed my job to finish my graduate program. I was hurt, but I wasn't stupid. I declined the offer. After a short conversation with no booty call, I went home.

My body was weak. My mind was weak. My soul was weak. I wanted to hide. I didn't want to see or talk to anybody. I was scared that if I revealed what had happened, my weak ass wouldn't be able to recover. EVER! There was so much that I needed to say to my ex. There were so many questions. Why me? Why did you put me through this? How am I ever going to trust a man again? How will I ever face the embarrassment of telling people who ask if I'm okay that I'm not because he chose to stick his dick where it didn't belong?

Well, that day came when my field advisor asked what was going on with me. She knew something was off, and I didn't want to tell her.

"Where's your ring?" She asked while in supervision.

At that moment, my eyes started to water, and I broke down. As I tried to pull myself together by wiping my eyes with a balled up tissue, I finally answered.

"I'm not getting married anymore."

She sat silently while I cried. She had been married for almost thirty years, so I wasn't expecting her to know how I felt. She didn't offer advice. She just let me vent and tell her how I felt. She knew I was hurt. She was like a mother figure to me, so even though she didn't say much, I knew she wanted to just sit on the floor and let me lay my head across her lap while she stroked my head. I felt embarrassed crying in front of her - in front of anybody who wanted to know what happened.

Because I was hurt and embarrassed, things quickly turned to a dark place. I never thought I would ever say I hated someone, but I hated him with every inch of my body. I was scared that if I saw him again, I would kill him. I finally realized how Bernadine from *Waiting to Exhale* could put all her husband's clothes in the car and light it on fire after she found out he left her for another woman. I was ready to burn down the city.

As the days slowly went by at work, my heart still ached. However, I wasn't in this alone. My coworker had been through the same thing. She was engaged and called it off. She was hurt too, but she was big on faith. I admired her for that. She came to work every day holding her head up high telling me it was going to be okay. I wanted to believe her. I wanted to snap my fingers to fix my broken heart and confidence. It just wasn't happening fast enough. I started to notice that I wasn't sleeping, and I couldn't eat. Dark circles began to form under my eyes, and I had no desire to go anywhere but home. My coworker encouraged me to see a counselor.

Caught off guard, I responded, "A counselor?!"

With certainty, she replied, *"Yes, why not? They pay for it through work! I loved my counselor! She helped me see a lot of things that I overlooked about my relationship and my past. Just try it out. The agency won't know why you went, but they just know that you used the services."*

"Well, do you have the number?"

"Yep! Let me write it down for you! I'm telling you this will be good for you."

As I looked at the number, I exhaled very slowly. I didn't want to admit that I needed to talk to someone other than my friends, but it was necessary. I had another year of school to get through, and I had my first book in the process of being published in less than three months. Going through a heartbreak was the last thing I needed to stop me from moving forward with my goals. If anyone were to help me, it had to be someone who didn't know me, right?

***

I arrived at my first counseling session not knowing what to expect. It was like reverting to being a child on their first day of school. I was scared as shit. I didn't know what she was going to ask, and I was determined not to cry. I wanted to let her know I was okay even though that was a bold-face lie. I walked through the glass doors. To my left was a wooden door. I opened it and stepped into a small waiting area. A blonde woman with piercing blue eyes wearing glasses came out and told me she would be with me in a minute. My hair was thrown up on top of my head, and I was dressed like a homeless person. Disheveled was an understatement.

As another person came out of her office, I sat there looking around the room. There were another small couch and a couple of chairs with a water cooler between them. It seemed very grandma-like. The walls were wooden, and the couches and chairs were not up-to-date. I wanted to get a sip of the water. But, it was my first time there, so I didn't want to seem too anxious by getting water. She motioned for me to come into her office and have a seat. She had pictures hung on the wall. Among those pictures was her license to counsel. She seemed to be very pleasant and smiled when I sat down, which made me feel warm. I needed warmth.

She introduced herself stating she was a nurse and social worker. At that point, I was reassured that if I had a heart attack from explaining my not-so-happily-ever-after, she was going to save me physically and emotionally. She said she was from around the area. That made me somewhat uneasy. I didn't want to see her out anywhere because technically she was a stranger, and I hate when strangers know my business. I hate when anyone knows my business. As she continued to speak about her longevity in the helping profession, she was surprised to know I was getting my master's in social work. I'm sure she felt like she was on the spot and thought I would be judging her interviewing and intervention skills. Luckily for her, I was too heartbroken to care.

"What brings you in today? Tell me what's going on?"

"Girl, let me tell you!!!! This motherfucker ruined my fucking life!!!! That's currently what's going on and why I'm here!!!!"

Although that's what I wanted to say, those words never came out of my mouth. Instead, in a low, shaky voice, I said, "I'm here because I was engaged, but the wedding was called off."

"Why was it called off?"

Silence...

As the tears came down my face, I finally spoke. "I found out he was with another woman while we were engaged. On top of that, he gave me an STD."

More silence…

"Oh, honey, I am sorry to hear that!"

At this point, I couldn't control my tears. I was wiping my face with the sleeve of my raggedy black jacket that I was wearing. She told me there was tissue next to me and that I could use them so I wouldn't have to use the sleeve of my jacket. I eventually picked up a tissue and began to use it to wipe my puffy eyes.

"Did you confront him about the other woman?"

"Yes, I did. I texted him. He never responded."

"What about the STD? Does he know you have it?"

With more tears in my eyes, I replied, "Yes, he knows. We weren't intimate the first half of our relationship because he was overseas. When he came home, we had our first sexual encounter. I had an immediate physical reaction in my genital area."

With of a look of validation, I knew the counselor was not able to tell me I got it from him. However, she gave me confidence that I was right. After all, she was a nurse. As the session went on, she asked me about how my mood had been since everything happened. I told her that I was trying to stay busy since I was in school. However, I did not want to involve myself in much social activity because I was embarrassed about everything. I let her know my appetite had gone down, and it was difficult for me to sleep. I did reassure her that I was still going to work every day, and I continued to stay on top of my school work. She applauded me for staying focused in such a tough time of my life.

It was almost my birthday, and I thought if I attended the six counseling sessions that were covered by the agency, I would surely be okay by then. As I mentioned before, I had never cried over a man. Anything longer than a week was an issue for me. Unfortunately, it was going on three months for this dickhead. As I was creeping up on my fifth session of counseling, the unthinkable happened. It was 1:47 a.m. and my phone's screen lit up notifying me of a message that had just come through. This was no ordinary text message. This was a message through a video app. He and I used this app frequently when he was stationed overseas. This was our way of seeing each other. I would always get butterflies during our calls. Well, there were no butterflies this time. Furthermore, the conversation was far worse than I could ever have imagined it to be.

I immediately opened the message thinking, *wait 'til I tell this motherfucker what's on my mind.* I didn't know why I needed to tell him anything. The damage was already done. At this point, his number and social media accounts were blocked. However, I forgot about this video app. It didn't matter though. I was supposed to hate this asshole with every fiber of my body. Why would I open a damn message from him*? Damn!* Unfortunately, I was not able to release my rage because it wasn't him. It was worse! It was the girl he left me for. Now, most women in my circumstance would have gone the hell off on this chick. But, I read the first message and things instantly changed. My heart was beating fast as I read her message.

"*Hi. I am the girlfriend of your ex, and I am three months pregnant with his child. I am having a hard time with him, and I'm reaching out to you for help. Please send me a message back if you get this.*"

I closed out the message instantly. I had come so far in my counseling sessions, and I was refusing to go back to square one. She sent another message. *Dammit! I forgot that if you read a message the person can see it. Dammit! Dammit! Dammit!* It didn't take a rocket scientist to know that. Apparently, I was the exception to the rule. I opened the second message.

"Please! I need your help. I have a daughter, and he gets upset when he gets drunk. I don't know what to do. Can you please tell me anything that you know?"

Inhale. Slow exhale. This shit cannot be real!

As I tried to gather what thought process I had left, I was at a point where I was tired. Physically. Mentally. Emotionally. I had no anger to give to this woman. None. I knew I was making progress and moving in the right direction when I decided to go to counseling. I had things to do. I had places to go and new people to meet. I couldn't let this hold me back any longer. Most importantly, the closure I felt that I needed before was gone. Even though I didn't get answers from him, she was going to give me that closure so I could finally rest.

"I'm not sure what information you want from me… He was an engaged man when you decided to be with him."

"I never knew he was engaged. He told me y'all broke up before he came back from overseas

because you cheated on him. When did you guys break up? How long have y'all been together?"

"He lied to you. That's the same story he told me about his ex-wife. We've been together since July 2014. We went on vacation together right before Christmas, and I've been coming to visit him every month since he got back to the States. We broke up at the end of April."

"Well, he asked me to be his girlfriend in February on Valentines' Day weekend. That was also the weekend of my daughter's birthday, and he got her everything she needed. When did you guys get engaged?"

"We got engaged in February, a week before Valentine's Day. How did you guys meet?"

"I met him before he came back from overseas. He and my dad worked together, and that's how I know him. I just don't know what to do. He always picks fights whenever he starts drinking and says he will change. I am having his child, and I have a daughter of my own. I have no one out here with me, and I want to go back home to my family. His mother told me to leave him."

As much as I wanted to tell her, "*Bitch this isn't my problem,*" I had to keep it real with her.

"If you are having issues with someone who has lied from the beginning to both you and me, where do you think your relationship will end up? You have a daughter. Is this the person you want to raise your kid? He needs help, and things are not going to change if he doesn't get the help he needs. If you want me to be completely honest with you, he's hiding other things from you, too. But, I'll let him tell you."

"What is it?"

Five-second pause…

"He has an STD, and I'm sure he didn't tell you."

"No, he didn't tell me. Now, I'm sitting here crying and don't know what to do."

"Well, how did you end up finding me on here?"

"I'm on his iPad."

Silence…

"I'm going to tell my dad what he has done to me."

"Good luck with everything."

That was the end. That was it. That's how my happily ever after came to an end. Still, I needed one more thing before I could put everything to rest. I needed my wedding dress back. I'm sure most women probably would burn their wedding dress, but I felt it meant something to me. Of course, spending $1800 was enough to keep it, but it represented something I had never felt or saw before from another man. And, that was love. Yes, it may have been fake love in his book. But, for me it was real. It was the first time I thought I had deserved to be married and have a partner who equally cared for and supported me as I did them.

All my life I've witnessed the women around me become single mothers and never get married. Marriage was something I never saw in my future, and I wasn't pushing for it. However, when the opportunity presented itself, I felt different for the first time. I felt admired for the first time. I felt like someone loved me because of my work ethic, bubbly personality, and my desire to be successful. I wanted that feeling back - not from him. I needed it back in any form I could get it. That feeling was in my wedding dress.

I had left my wedding dress with his sister. At the time of our break-up, I couldn't bring myself to visit the small town where they lived and where the dress was purchased. I was hurt. I knew I wouldn't be able to look at the dress without crying… or setting it on fire. After a few weeks of trying to contact her with little to no communication, I became enraged! I began to think his sister was a con artist just like her shitty-ass brother by keeping my dress and ignoring my messages.

"I've tried to contact you several times to get my dress. I am not sure what is going on, but if I do not receive my dress back, then I will contact the local authorities to retrieve my wedding dress."

Within ten minutes, she finally responded, *"I've been busy with interviews, and our grandmother fell. So, I apologize, but for you to involve the police, that's just cruel."*

I thought to myself, *how the fuck am I cruel when I've been sending your ass messages for three weeks informing you of times and dates I was available with no reply? Oh okay! But, you respond when I threaten you with the police! Bitch, you tried it!*

With a deep breath, I calmly replied, "I apologize. I am not sure who and what to believe. I just want my dress back so I can move on with my life."

Thirty minutes later, his mother messaged me. *Let's just slow down and take a deep breath. Let me know when you are available, and I will bring you your dress."*

Thinking again, *that's what the fuck I thought!*

I replied, "That will be fine. I can meet you Monday at your job. I am off."

"Okay, that is fine. We can meet on my lunch break."

That Monday was my twenty-ninth birthday. I arrived at the breakfast café wearing a black summer dress. Black represented death to me, and I wanted to make sure he and his family were dead to me once I got my dress back and left that café. I walked in and saw his mother sitting at a table wearing her work clothes, which consisted of scrubs. She was a dental hygienist.

"Hello, how are you doing?" she said.

"I'm okay. Yourself?"

I didn't want her to know it was my birthday. I didn't want her to question me on why I would meet her on a day I should be celebrating. If she had asked, I wouldn't have had an answer. The waiter came to the table and took our order. I didn't order anything big. My appetite was non-existent. Once the waiter left with our order, the last and dreadful conversation began.

"Have you spoken to him?"

"No, I haven't after asking for the money back for the down payment on the venue and bridesmaids' dresses."

"I asked him about the ring. He claimed he didn't have it, so I told him one of y'all are lying. When I asked again, he wouldn't look at me, which is normally when I can tell he's lying."

"Well, I don't have the ring. I sent it back. I did get a message from his girlfriend who reached out to me last week asking for help. She stated she is pregnant and doesn't know what she's going to do because your son picks fights with her when he's drunk. She said she didn't have any family with her and would contact her dad once I told her your son has an STD he seemingly forgot to mention."

"Well, I found out she's a big liar as well. She has a lot of conflicting stories."

"What do you mean?"

"She told us she did not speak to her father and her mother, but they went up to visit them for a month because she threatened to leave him. When she came to our house, she and my son would be smoking weed and leave her daughter at my house. I mean, who leaves their daughter with a family they hardly know? They would medicate her at night, and she wouldn't even be sick. It was troubling. I told him he had to leave and it was too soon to be with someone else. She is not welcomed back into my home."

"Well, she's pregnant now, so congrats on the new addition. He tried to force me to have a kid before marriage, but I refused."

At this point, I had to let her know just how fucked up her son was.

"Well, I believe she's not pregnant either. She lies a lot. The last time I spoke with him, he said there were no changes with her body at all. Nothing. On top of that, she told us she was a nurse, but later found out she's a convicted felon working as a cashier."

As bad as I wanted to say out loud, "He left me for a bum bitch," I refrained and remained quiet. At the end of breakfast, his mother paid for our meals, and we walked out to her new white Cherokee truck. I thanked her for paying for my meal while she unlocked her trunk and pulled out a big puffy pink bag. I couldn't believe I was a touching the bag that held my wedding dress. It had been almost six months since I tried it on at the boutique. Still wearing her sunglasses, she placed it in my arms.

With her voice trembling, she said, *"Here ya go."*

I could see her cheeks turn red. She was hurt. She knew this was the end. She knew I didn't deserve this. She knew her son wasn't shit for what he did. She knew my replacement didn't measure up, and she was uncertain if she was ever going to go away. I hugged her and thanked her for giving me back my dress.

With a single tear rolling down her red cheek, she said, *"You take care of yourself."*

With tears in my eyes, I replied, "I will. Thank you."

And, with that, I put my dress in the trunk and drove off, never looking back to one of the most painful six months of my life. Happy birthday to me!

Mission II: Sunshine

After my birthday, I started getting back into the club scene. I decided to go out with my girlfriends at the time to shake off my dark days. It was nerve-wracking. I didn't know if I was ready, but I damn sure was going to try. Since my appetite had not bounced back yet, weight dropped off my body fast. Dresses I would normally not feel comfortable wearing due to having a small pouch began to appear more appealing and fitting to my body. One of those dresses was a coral sundress that appeared to make my body look slim. It had a low V-cut in the front, which permitted me to wear a white necklace to draw attention to my cleavage. Attention is what I wanted, and attention is what I got.

One night, a guy walked through the crowd wearing a grey t-shirt. His hair was combed back, and his teeth were so white and straight that I thought they were fake. We made eye contact, and then he winked and smiled. He was the sexiest man I had ever seen. He didn't look familiar. Since I am from a small town, when someone is that good-looking, we all know about it. I didn't know him though. I smiled back, thinking it would go no further. I was wrong.

He walked over and said in a heavy accent, *"You are pretty."*

While smiling back, I said, "Thank you," and looked around at all my friends who were staring at us both.

As he leaned in very close to my face, almost touching my cheek, he said, *"Wanna dance?"*

"Sure. Why not?"

After spending what felt like an eternity on the dancefloor, I returned to my table of friends who were in awe of how good-looking this foreign man was. Honestly, I was, too. He looked too perfect and looked as though he stepped out of a magazine. He returned to my table after buying drinks at the bar with my friends and me. He continued to tell me I was pretty. He couldn't say many words in English, but that didn't matter since all I wanted to do was look at him. However, he had other plans. Before I knew it, the unthinkable happened. He kissed me on the mouth! Although, I was caught off guard, I was okay with a little bit of tongue and lip action. Besides, I hadn't kissed anyone in the past six months, so what did I have to lose?

At first, nothing appeared to be a big deal. I liked the attention. Especially from a beautiful foreign man with the perfect smile, teeth, and body to go with a heavy accent. It made me feel good again. It made me feel like I was slowly healing and would finally be okay with dating again. While he asked if he could come back home with me, I was more curious to know why a man so good-looking was in my hometown.

"I play soccer. Can you take me back to campus in the morning? My bus leaves in the morning."

Although his communication was a significant barrier, I understood that whatever happened tonight would be forgotten once he was on his way back to his homeland.

I replied, "Sure, I guess."

As he grabbed my hand, we began walking toward the exit. My friends couldn't believe I had bagged the foreign guy!

With giggles and big smiles, they asked, *"Bitch, are you really taking him home with you?!"*

I gave a big grin and said, "YEP!"

We stopped at the gas station and picked up condoms. I had never been more embarrassed. I know it was the right thing to do, but I kept thinking, *are you really at a gas station getting condoms because you're about to have a one-night stand with some sexy foreign guy?* I guess so.

When we got back into the car, he asked again in broken English, *"Will you take me to campus in the morning?"*

Slightly annoyed, I said, "Yes!"

As I opened my apartment door and let us in, I immediately felt regret. I didn't want to do this anymore. I didn't know this man. Yes, I knew I wouldn't see him ever again, but I felt uneasy. I felt sick to my stomach. I just wanted to take him to the campus right then. I think I made a mistake. No, let's try that again. I don't think I made a mistake. I did make a mistake. As I walked up the steps and set my purse down on my living room stand, he immediately began to get undressed and pulled me closer to him. He started kissing me aggressively in the mouth. I was turned off. I felt disgusting. His sexy smile, body, and white teeth were suddenly unattractive. I knew this was not going to end well for him.

"Take clothes off baby."

"I will. Just slow down."

As I slipped off my coral dress and took off my white necklace, I noticed he was already naked with the condom on. I did not want to go forward with having sex with him. Unfortunately, I did not know if he would turn violent if I said no. I played myself and ultimately played him. I laid down on my living room floor while he climbed on top of me. Things got aggressive very quickly. He grabbed my hair very tightly and aggressively began to shove his tongue down my throat. He pretty much licked the makeup off my face, making me feel like a piece of meat. After five minutes of choking on his tongue, hard pounding, pulling my hair that place my head in an awkward position that began to hurt, and my genital area feeling dry as a desert, I was done. I immediately told him to stop. I couldn't do it anymore.

"What? I almost done baby."

Embarrassed, I replied, "I can't do this!"

"Can you jack me off or give head?

I replied aggravatedly, "No, I just can't do this!"

With a look of concern, he asked, "You no satisfied?"

Knowing he wouldn't understand, I tried to explain. "No, I just got of a relationship. I was engaged to be married, and it didn't work out. I thought I was ready, but I'm not."

Now he had the look of confusion. "You married?"

I was back to being frustrated. "No, I was engaged to be married. Forget it. I will take you back to the campus."

As we got in the car, I felt the walk of shame. Normally, I wouldn't care, but this was different. I was trying to go back to my old ways of being single and carefree, but it backfired. Hard. In addition, things got worse. I asked him how old he was.

"I twenty-three."

He looked almost thirty. He had a full beard. Although, it did make sense why I was taking him to a college campus.

"Why don't you have a girlfriend?"

"Yes, I do."

My stomach dropped to my toes. This *motherfucker* has a girlfriend? How did I run into another one of these guys? A cheater. I should have asked this question in the beginning. But, when someone asks to come home with me, I assume they are single. I guess I was wrong. I realized I am too gullible and should up my radar when bullshit comes my way. The conversation continued.

"Do you have children?"

"Yes, have two children."

Then, he proceeded to show me a picture of them on his phone as his screensaver. So not only was the sex terrible, this foreign guy is a cheater. He cheated on his girlfriend and ultimately turned his back on his kids. Damn. It's a cold world. We arrived at the campus. Before getting out of the car, he leaned over and kissed me on the cheek.

"You satisfied, right?"

With an annoyed but calm tone, I said, "Yeah."

I got back home and took off my coral dress again. One dress I felt confident in quickly turned into the dress I never wanted to see or wear again. The next day, my girlfriend called me.

"So, how was that sexy dude you took home?"

With my head hanging low, I said, "I just couldn't do it."

"Why? What happened?"

With my head still hanging and tone low, I answered, "I just didn't feel comfortable. Yeah, he was good-looking, but I'm not ready. I thought I was, but I'm not."

"It's okay. With everything that has happened to you in these last few months, I understand."

Did my friends really understand? This was different. I had never felt so low in my life. I didn't know when this feeling was going to end. I realized this was a nightmare I didn't want my worst enemy to go through. Life was tough at this moment, and I needed a solution quick. It was time for me to move, and I was ready for a change. I couldn't bare living in my one-bedroom apartment knowing he had been in here. I wanted to go fast.

The new place I found was in a bigger community with townhouses, apartments, and a clubhouse. It was in a good neighborhood, and the two bedrooms and two baths were a plus. In addition to that, I had a garage and a storage space downstairs. I was moving up and on with my life. I was refusing to stay stagnant. Once I signed my papers, I was off to a fresh start. So, I thought.

I moved in and got settled. My family came over, and we ordered dinner. It felt good to be loved for the moment. It felt good to be celebrated by the ones you loved. I was on a high. I thought everything would be smooth sailing from there on out. Well, it wasn't until after everyone left that I realized nothing changed but my location. Although school kept me busy momentarily, I struggled to get proper sleep. I was having nightmares about my failed engagement and would routinely wake up in the middle of the night almost in tears. It was like I was being attacked and didn't know how to stop it. Everywhere I went, I was triggered. Especially by bald heads and black trucks. It was painful. I couldn't take it anymore. My weekend program at school and writing my first book was a temporary fix. Still, I needed to get away. Fast.

Fortunately, after living in my apartment for two months, one of my male best friends was getting married, and his bachelor party was going to be in Miami. I went to Miami a few years back with an old friend. Although we never went out to the bars, the sand and sun were beautiful. We encountered people from different ethnic backgrounds speaking different languages. I could not wait to return; however, I didn't know when and with whom I would return. The day came when I spoke to my male best friend on the phone.

"Hey man, what you up to?"

"Nothing. Just getting ready to go on this Miami trip. A couple of my guys are throwing my bachelor's party in Miami."

"I love Miami! When are y'all going?"

"We're leaving the weekend of September 25th. We got our flights cheap, too."

The bachelor party was the same weekend I was supposed to get married. At the time, I had no plans on how I was going to fill that day with activities, so Miami appeared to be the next best option.

Hoping for an invite, I said, "Man, I wish I could come. I love Miami so much. Plus, I need a getaway."

Excitedly, he said, *"Man, you should come! We 'bout to have a good time!"*

"You think your friends are going to care if I come? I will be the only girl there."

"Naw, they won't care. Everyone that's going to be there, you already know. They'll be good. As long as you have your own money, we straight!"

That's all I needed to hear. I quickly got off the phone and started looking up cheap flights to Miami. I was spending my wedding day where there was nothing to see but sand and sunshine. I started looking through all my bathing suits and outfits I wanted to wear. I wanted to make sure I was going to live it up in Miami. Nothing was going to stop me from having an enjoyable time. Not even heartbreak.

I went to work the next day, put in my request to be off, and was quickly approved. It was on! Miami was going to see me again, except with a different mindset. I was going there with no fucks given. I needed to bounce back, and this was going to be my hard comeback. I had something to prove to myself. I didn't want to be defeated anymore. I was going to have fun and be carefree. Luckily for me, I could get on the same flight as the bachelor crew. However, they were nowhere to be found at the airport when I arrived. So, I began to send text messages to ensure they would be arriving soon because I was almost ready to board.

"Where are you guys?"

"We are coming. Some of the guys were late when I had to pick them up! We're coming, man!

Since I was still waiting to board, I figured they would be at the airport soon, and there would be no hassle. Well, I was wrong. As time came closer to board, I kept sending more text messages. My anxiety was starting to grow because it was a possibility I was traveling to Miami by myself.

Panicked, I texted again, "Where the hell are y'all? We are boarding!"

"We got stopped by the cops for speeding. We are coming! Tell the desk person to hold the plane!"

I thought to myself; *Really? You want me to have them hold the plane for y'all black asses, knowing y'all should have been here on time?* I was beyond annoyed and knew that when these people close the door, that was it. I was going to Miami by myself. Before I hopped on the plane, I stopped at the desk.

"Ma'am, four more people are coming. I'm not sure if you can hold out a few more minutes, but they wanted you to know they will be here."

Her smile seemed reassuring as she said, *"Ok."*

As I sat down in my seat, I thought, *Am I really going to Miami alone? How am I going to get to the hotel? I'll just take an Uber, right?* Luckily, after sitting on the plan for five minutes deep in thought trying to map out how I was going to get from the airport to my hotel, I spotted four black guys boarding the plan. I knew all but one of them. I was furious as I gave them a strong side eye.

"'Bout fucking time!"

They ignored me and kept walking to their seat. Two hours later, we were in Miami. While walking through Miami Airport, one of the groomsmen asked a question I readily wanted to answer.

"Y'all ready to turn up this weekend!?"

"Of course! I was supposed to get married tomorrow."

Two of the groomsmen said with shock and confusion in their voices, "You're supposed to get married tomorrow? What?!"

"Yes, I was. It didn't work, so now I'm here!"

"Good shit! Now, let's turn up!"

That's all I needed to hear. I was in turn up mode, and all bets were off. I didn't care what happened that weekend. I was with a bunch of guys, and I knew they were well informed on how to turn up and have a good time. We got to our hotel, and I was super anxious to get the festivities going. We went and picked up the rental car. It was the new Tahoe truck, which seated up to seven people. Once everything was paid for, we hopped into the truck with the music blasting on our way to South Beach.

When we arrived at the hotel, I was excited to drop my luggage off and get out into the streets of Miami. Unfortunately, we were so excited that we didn't realize we came to the wrong hotel. Even worse, I charged a room to my credit card. What a disaster. However, the receptionist told me she could remove the charge from my card. I was lucky. After going ten minutes down the street, we finally arrived at the correct hotel. I checked in and headed to my room. I set my suitcase on my bed and opened the curtains. It was bright and sunny, and the water was beautiful. I couldn't wait to hang out with good people and enjoy the beach.

I told myself this weekend I was refusing to cry. I was going to be okay. I wasn't going to sulk in my sorrow or let anyone see me sweat. This was a time for celebration for my friend and his love for his soon-to-be wife. I had to be happy. There was no other choice. This weekend was all about him, and he didn't deserve me being around him with a bad attitude or sadness. He needed fun, laughs, and reassurance that he was making one of the best decisions of his life. I was going to make sure that was going to happen.

I changed clothes and went down to their room. They had music playing and bottles popping. They were ready to let loose, and so was I. We sat around and laughed, and then explored the hotel. I stumbled across a bar located in their lobby area. I never paid it any attention but was sure I would return to it the next day. I needed to make sure I was highly intoxicated by noon. As night crept upon us, it was time to figure out where we were going and what I was going to wear. I decided I would go with a simple look. I wore a blueish pants romper that required me to wear a sticky bra since the romper top half was a halter top. I didn't feel my best, but it was going to do for the night.

It was hot and sticky so I should have known better than to wear pants in Miami. Once the guys got dressed, we headed downstairs to snap photos. Then, we were off to the club. Regrettably, what we thought was going to be a turn-up night was going to be easily shut down my Miami Police Department. When we arrived at the first club, it was forty dollars to get in for girls and sixty dollars for guys. I almost choked. I had never paid over twenty dollars to get into a bar. I found it completely insane to pay that much money to sip on one or two drinks and listen to music that is probably downloaded on my phone. It didn't matter anyway because once the guys got to the front door to pay, they did not meet dress code rules.

Apparently, in Miami South Beach, men can wear pants not shorts. When I turned around to see who all had on shorts, every one of them had on shorts but one. So, half of them had to go back to the hotel to change. My best friend and his best man decided they would not go back to the hotel.

They would just find a nearby store instead. This store run was going to change our lives forever.

As we split up, I decided I didn't need to go back to the hotel and would just go along for the ride to the nearby stores. We had little time, so we sped through the streets. At one point, we were driving so fast, the best man hit a bump in the road, and my whole body hit the ceiling of the car. No lie! Each store we went to was bad luck. The first store we went to only sold groceries. We were so confused because this store is one of the biggest chains in the country. It sells everything under the sun, yet the one store we went to only sold groceries. Epic fail!

As we continued our search, the next store was closed. By this time, it was almost 3:00 a.m., and we were still riding around looking for a store that was open. We finally arrived at a store that was open and appeared to sell what we needed - men's pants. We hopped out the car while it was running and went into the store to find pants that would meet the dress code. When we returned to the car, my heart dropped to my feet. The best man, who was driving us, was surrounded by police. His hands were in the air, and his newly bought pants were over his left shoulder. *Did they think he stole the pants because they are not in a bag?* I had no clue what to expect nor did I know what we did wrong.

As we approached the best man while other police officers were getting out of the car, I heard the officer ask aggressively, *"Did you know this was a stolen car?"*

The best man replied, "No, I didn't. This our rental car we got today."

As I watched the cops surround the truck and open the door while using their flashlights, I was hoping we wouldn't get killed. It's one thing to get pulled over for speeding. It's another thing when you're being accused of riding around in a stolen car. All I could think about was that I was with two black males, and it didn't matter what we were in Miami celebrating. We were headed toward being the next hashtag. We continued to plead with the police that we were out-of-towners and that my best friend was getting married next week. We couldn't let him die that night!

"Do y'all have proof of where y'all got this truck from?"

The best man responded, "Yeah, it's in the glove compartment in the truck."

As he hopped in the front passenger seat, the police officer was flashing a light to ensure no mysterious firearms were lingering around. I was praying and hoping those papers would pop up. It was getting late, my armpits were sweaty, and it was hot as hell outside. I felt like this was never going to end and that it was taking entirely too long to find those papers. Then, I saw the expression of *what the fuck* written on the best man's face. He had left the rental contract paper in his back pants pocket. His pants were at the hotel with the other groomsmen. I quickly grabbed my phone, unlocked the screen, and made a phone call to the other groomsmen back at the hotel.

I frantically said, "Aye, can y'all take a picture of the rental contract and text it to me? It's in the best man's back pocket of his pants."

With confusion in his voice, the second groomsmen replied, *"Yeah, why wassup? What happened?"*

"We got stopped by the police in the truck, and they're saying our truck is stolen."

"WHAT?! FOR REAL?! What y'all gon' do?!"

Unfortunately, we were shit out of luck. After receiving the picture message of the rental contract and receipt, the best man was advised by the police to call the car rental place. While he was on hold, the police did verify the license plates were stolen. By this time, the police supervisor had arrived with a few dogs. Surprisingly, she was a woman. When I took a moment to calm my nerves, I realized the three officers who arrived first were diverse. There was one Caucasian male, one African American male, one Hispanic male, and the supervisor who was a Hispanic female. They were pretty chill once they were convinced we didn't know we were driving around in a stolen vehicle.

"Where are y'all from?"

"We're from Ohio."

"What y'all doing all the way down here from Ohio?"

The groom replied, "It's my bachelor party weekend. I'm getting married next week."

The Hispanic male cop began to laugh, *"And, she let yo' ass come to Miami for your bachelor's party?!"*

Everyone began to laugh. There was no more anxiety. It was all good.

The cop turned toward me. *"Wait! If it's a bachelor's party, what are you doing here with the fellas?"*

Quickly responding with no shame, I responded, "I was supposed to get married tomorrow, but I'm not. So, I decided to celebrate my best friend's bachelor's party with him and his friends."

I could have lied and just said I was there to hang out, but for whatever reason, I felt compelled to blurt out my wedding was not happening anymore. Looking back I think I was trying to tell myself I was going to be fine even though I was not getting married the next day. I had to hear myself say it out loud. I am not getting married. I am not getting married. I AM NOT GETTING MARRIED. The more I said it out loud, the faster it became a reality. I was going to get through this weekend with no setbacks.

The police supervisor pulled us all together and made a very clear point.

"You all were lucky tonight. You could have been killed for driving in a stolen car. When you return the car, give them hell for being negligent."

Before leaving, we asked the officer, "By the way, how did y'all know this car was stolen anyway? This car was parked in a store parking lot."

She replied, *"When y'all drove through one of our traffic lights, it scanned the license plates and hit back to our police department as a stolen vehicle."*

I thought to myself, *damn, the way we were speeding through the streets, we would have for sure been dead.*

"Unfortunately, y'all won't be able to drive this car. Do y'all got anyone who can come pick y'all up?"

"Yeah, we got some people to call. The car isn't big enough though. How are we all going to be able to fit?"

"Technically, y'all can drive the truck back to the hotel with no license plates on it. You can get pulled over for it, but they can't put y'all in jail. Remember, let the rental place know because of their negligent services, they should reimburse y'all."

In unison, we sternly said, "Oh, don't worry! We will!"

It was 4:45 a.m. by the time police left the scene, and the other groomsmen arrived in their four-door Sudan. I jumped into the car and started immediately explaining to them what happened. They were flabbergasted. We pulled around to the truck where my male best and his best man was sitting.

"So, what y'all wanna do?"

Surprisingly, the groom still wanted to go out to the bar.

"Man, I wanna go out! This is my weekend! I'm not gone let this bullshit ruin it!"

We were forty-five minutes away from the hotel, so it was pointless to go back since the bar we wanted to go to was going to close in an hour. We took our chances to go out bar hopping. No license plates equaled no jail time. That sounded good to me. Unfortunately, not everyone was down to go out. We arrived back at the bar that had the strict dress code. Unbeknownst to us, you had to have reservations to get into the bar - even though the bar was closing in an hour. This was probably the worse news yet. The other groomsmen became irritated and told the groom, best man, and me they were going back to the hotel. As we walked back to the car, we decided to turn back around and attempt to get in any way. We did not go through all this and come all this way to be turned away. The best man approached the counter.

"Man, you mean to tell me with the bar closing in an hour, we can't get in?"

With boredom in his tone, the bouncer said, "Naw, you have to have reservations."

"We didn't know that. It's my man's bachelor party weekend, and we just wanted to get in somewhere really quick to celebrate."

"Aight, forty dollars for you; sixty dollars for them."

We paid our money and walked in. There were flashing lights and women standing on cement blocks in the middle of the bar dancing on each other. There were a lot of people drinking, laughing, smoking, and everything else under the sun. The DJ was yelling on the mic getting everyone fired up! We made our way closer to the bar. Because I had been standing outside for the past two hours, I had sweated out my outfit, and my sticky bra was no longer sticking. I had to hold my arms up to hide my lopsided breasts. It didn't dawn on me that I was in Miami, and it would have been perfectly fine for me to go braless.

Although I wanted to change my outfit, what I really wanted was water. I felt dehydrated. I knew the drinks would be expensive so, I had no other choice but to pay eleven dollars for bottled water. I wasn't pleased about the price, but after the night I had been through, I had to suck up that eleven dollars. I looked around the club as people walked by. The women all had big asses and big boobs. Everybody in Miami appeared to put extra effort into their appearance. I really couldn't blame them. They saw the sun and beach every day. I'm not sure how relationships lasted down here. Everyone was attractive.

After drinking half of my bottled water, I had to go the bathroom. Before going in, I saw an attractive woman standing in the entryway. She had on a neon orange skirt with a matching top. Her waist was as skinny as my arm, and her hair was to her ass. She was with a group of girls, and they were all equally attractive. I continued to walk past her and went to the restroom. When I returned, a guy who was freakishly tall walked past wearing a brown Yogi Bear hat. He startled me because he was so tall. Once his face hit the light, he looked familiar. He looked like a professional athlete, but I wasn't for sure.

I walked back over to the groom and best man. They were still standing in the same spot. The freakishly tall guy walked back by, went over to the DJ, and stood next to the girl wearing the orange neon outfit and her friends. She was pretty, so I expected her to pull someone like that. As I continued to stare at them, the DJ laid all my assumptions to rest. It turns out the freakishly tall guy was a professional athlete who had just signed a major NBA deal. The DJ held up the mic and announced who he was and what team he was going to play for during the upcoming season. I guess an hour and forty bucks was worth it after all.

As we exited the building, the groom was still not ready to go back to the hotel, so we continued to explore. The next bar we went to had extended hours. It was open until 9:00 a.m. I thought, *who in their right mind would be partying until 9:00 a.m.?* Apparently, a lot of people because to our surprise, when we got the okay to enter, it was filled with people. There were no flashing lights and no hype DJ. There was just random music playing and everyone standing around sipping on their drinks.

It appeared to be an after-hour club and presented a chill vibe. We walked quickly through the crowd until we reached a back door. As we walked out, we attempted to go across the street to a strip club. We observed luxury cars outside this strip club, ranging from Maseratis to Bentleys. We knew we had the wrong strip club, and the people entering didn't look like us. On that note, it was time to head back to the hotel.

When we arrived at the hotel, I gathered my belongings and hopped out of the truck. The sun was coming up, so I was ready to get up to my room. Right before I went through the automatic doors to enter the hotel, another gray Tahoe truck arrived. A man got out and approached the best man. They exchanged words, and the man handed the best man a key. Then, the man got into the Tahoe truck with the stolen license plates lying in the back seat and drove away. I asked the best man how we got the new truck from the rental car place.

"I called and told them we would be at the hotel and they needed to bring us a different truck since the one they gave us was stolen in the system."

I nodded, turned around, and headed into the hotel. After entering my room, I slipped off my sweaty jumpsuit and threw my purse on the nightstand. I got into the bed naked and pulled the covers up to my face. Then, I turned toward the window and closed my eyes. The next day was coming, whether I liked it or not. I was prepared.

Section II:

"It is only when you are on the battlefield, your true friends are revealed."

-Games of Thrones

Mission III: Sixth Man off the Bench

I was awakened by the sun glaring through my window. The morning felt weird. I didn't want it to feel that way. It just did. I slid upward and sat up on the bed. I looked over at the window where I could see other tall buildings. I just sat there with a blank stare. I was trying not to think about anything. After staring outside for an extra three minutes, I scooted over to the side of the bed and looked at my phone. It was September 26, 2015. My wedding day. If someone had asked me eight months before that day, I would have never imagined telling someone I would be sitting in a hotel room in Miami staring out of a window. I should have been waking up to my hairstylist and makeup artist getting me ready. I should have been laughing and drinking mimosas with my girlfriends. My mom and grandmother should be bringing my wedding dress into my dressing room, ensuring it's free of wrinkles. This day should have been different. I quickly learned it wasn't, and it was never going to be.

I got up from the bed and went into the bathroom. I got into the shower and turned on steaming hot water. I wanted to feel fresh as if I had a fresh mindset. Once I left my hotel room, I didn't want to think about any wedding. I wanted to focus on myself and get the day started with drinks as soon as possible. Once I got dressed, I got onto the elevator and went down one floor to the groomsmen room. They were all dressed in basketball shorts and t-shirts. I didn't know what they were up to so I had to ask.

"What are y'all doing today?"

"We gon' try to hoop."

In a state of disgust, I said, "Really? We're in Miami and y'all are concerned about playing basketball?"

"Yeah."

Fortunately, one of the men who came along on the trip had no interest in going to play basketball.

"Well, I don't want to play basketball. You want to go get a drink instead?"

I had only met him the day before; however, I was stoked that he wanted to start the day of drinking because I knew I needed one. As we made our way downstairs, I remembered there was a bar attached to our hotel. It was a bit upscale, but I just wanted to get a drink. As we entered, we observed everyone in there to be dressed in their finest clothing. We felt out of place and didn't want to stay any longer than we should. We ordered two cranberry and vodkas. Once I felt a buzz, it was time for us to move on to the next place.

Everyone knows when you come to Miami, the beach is a must. As we left the hotel bar, we both agreed that we wanted to go to the beach to enjoy sun, alcohol, and water. I raced back up to my room and changed quickly into my two-piece hot pink swimsuit. That was what I needed - relaxation, an alcoholic drink, and a person who wanted to hang out to keep my mind off things. He did not know he was being used to keep my mind occupied, but I quickly found using him for his company was a wise decision.

I left my room and met him at his room. All the groomsmen were gone, so it was just us. He double-checked that he had all his belongings, and then off we went to the sandy beach. Because we were not able to drive our new rental truck, we chose to get an Uber that was willing to drive us to the beach from our hotel. Our first driver picked us up on the side of our hotel in his red Sudan. He appeared to have a heavy accent. But, with further conversation, we learned he lived in our home state before living in Miami. He was a cool and chill guy. That ride was worth every penny.

Ocean Boulevard is the place to be when going to Miami. All the shopping stores, restaurants, and beach are located within minutes of each other. This is the remarkable thing about Miami. If you had a sad day, you could get transported to Ocean Boulevard, and all your troubles would instantly disappear. That is what I was hoping for once I arrived. Sure enough, that's exactly what I got.

As we headed toward the beach while wearing my two-piece swimsuit and my orange net shirt, we passed a stand serving alcohol. We stopped and bought drinks. He ordered Long Island iced tea, and I had another cranberry and vodka. Since I hadn't eaten any breakfast, my buzz was still going from earlier, and this drink further kept me buzzed. I was feeling myself. I hadn't felt this good in a long time. I felt like all my pain was non-existent and nothing matter but my drink and the beach.

As we went out into the water, he and I began to get to know one another. We talked about how the dating world works, what we expect out of our significant other, and where we were in our current relationships. Luckily, by this time the few drinks I had in my system led me to tell my story without crying. I pretended that I had not been upset for the past six months. I acted as if my world had never crashed and burned. I let my toughness show. I was my shero.

We got out the ocean and dried off after snapping a few selfies. I was going to make this day seem as normal as possible. We put on our clothes and went back toward Ocean Boulevard. Then, we stood on the side of the road and called our Uber to have us transported back to the hotel. The first Uber we called was having difficulty finding us. There were so many people on the street. Instead of waiting for the Uber, we crossed the street. This time, I used my phone to get a different Uber to get us back to the hotel. As we followed the car and my GPS location map, we kept scanning the cars drive past. However, no one was pulling over to us. Then, my phone rang. It was the Uber guy.

"Hello, I am in a four-door CRV. Where are you located?"

"We are located across from Ocean Boulevard on the side of the street. I am in an orange net shirt."

Soon a blue-grayish CRV arrived. We hopped in and gave him the address to our hotel.

He wasn't as talkative as our last driver. It didn't matter to me anyway. I was starving and couldn't wait to get back to the hotel and change into my daisy dukes and eat with the groom and groomsmen. We got back to the hotel and quickly hopped out of the car. We ran to catch the elevator. I let him get off first and told him I would come back to his room when I was dressed to head out to eat.

I got off the elevator and went straight to my room. I threw off all my clothes and took a hot shower. I wanted to look pretty. I wanted to feel good about myself. I took my time putting on my makeup and looking at myself in the mirror longer than normal. I took deep breaths. Inhale. Exhale. I exited the bathroom and found my white tank top, daisy duke shorts that had rips on the pockets, and my Kimono. I slipped them on as fast as I could. As I arrived at the elevator, there was a hallway mirror to my left. I looked at my reflection one last time. *You got this.*

When I got to the guys' room, they were nowhere to be found. No one called me or texted me. I figured they were still playing basketball. However, the man I went to Ocean Boulevard with was dressed for dinner. It was just us again, so we caught the elevator back down to the lobby area and set out to find food. The air was comfortable. It looked as though it was going to rain, but I was hoping it would hold out since we didn't have the rental car and didn't want to get an Uber. We wanted to walk, and I was certainly okay with that.

As we made casual conversation, I noticed this guy was cool. I realized every time I was around him I had been laughing until my stomach hurt since we got to Miami. It was refreshing. He was very social and appeared to be having fun when I was around.

While walking, he stopped this random guy wearing a black suit jacket and asked, *"Hey! Where's a good place to get some food around here?"*

The guy didn't hesitate to tell us if we kept walking down the street, we would run into a Brazilian Steakhouse.

"Thank you, Sir!" he said with such enthusiasm.

After another five minutes of walking, we found the restaurant. There was no one inside but waitresses and waiters. We were the only guests there, which worked in our favor. As we were directed to sit down at a two-seater table, things changed very quickly. Suddenly, the staff started treating us differently. Apparently, since we came together, they automatically assumed we were a couple. Immediately, when we sat down, our waiter sat a candle in the middle of our table and lit it with a match.

"Let me set the mood for the couple this evening."

Not wanting to make our waiter feel embarrassed because his assumption of us being a couple was wrong, we giggled and let him proceed. He motioned his hand pointing to the salad bar, encouraging us to get appetizers. Once he walked away, we got up and went to the salad bar. We piled our plates with bread and finger foods. Those appetizers were some of the best I've ever had. While eating our appetizers and conversing about his relationship, the waiter returned with a slab of meat and a knife. He asked us if we wanted steak, and we both nodded yes. The waiter cut a couple of pieces of meat off and placed them on our plates. I bit into the meat, and it was the most tender, seasoned piece of meat that has ever touched my mouth. I was flabbergasted by the restaurant's over-the-top service and great food to match.

We continued to talk and laugh. The waiters continued to bring different meat for us to sample. They even brought over a bottle of wine. It was a fun experience. We had dessert to finish the meal. Although we talked about my shitty engagement ending and his breakups over the years, it felt good to vent and not feel like bursting into tears. In fact, we were having such an enjoyable time that we didn't realize the entire restaurant was full of people. We both turned and looked at each other and knew we came at the perfect time - before the dinner rush.

We left the restaurant and started wandering the streets again. We passed local shops and looked at all the rich people drive around in their luxurious foreign cars. The streets were crowded with traffic and the night was still young. A few hours had gone by, and we noticed all the walking was making us hungry again. So, we stopped at a local pizza shop. We continued to talk about could-have-been relationships. To my surprise, he wanted to be with a girl who was a redhead. He opened his phone and turned it around to show me their picture from high school. She had gorgeous blue eyes and was something you couldn't miss. He sounded like he wanted to marry her, but that opportunity has now passed. He said they are just friends now.

I wasn't going to show him a picture of my ex. By that time, I had erased every picture possible, so I didn't have to be reminded of the biggest mistake of my life. However, I did have a picture of my ring. It was four-carat princess cut. To this day, I kick myself in the foot because I sent it back to him. Although, I don't know what I would have done with it if I'd had kept it. I wouldn't wear it anymore, but for whatever reason, I regretted giving it back. Maybe I should've sold it? I guess I will never know.

We called the other guys and asked where they had been all day. They claimed they played basketball and went and picked up the last member of the bachelor party from the airport. She was a female, but she fit right in with the guys with her Jordans and fitted cap. We walked back to the hotel and went up to the groomsmen room. They had a stack of pizzas, and they were playing music while drinking liquor. We were headed to one of the most famous strip clubs in Miami. This was our last night there, so we had to make this night count. Before we headed off, the guys had become inquisitive about our whereabouts. They were petty as hell.

"So, what did y'all do all day?"

With a big smile, I said, "Oh, we went day drinking, and then to the ocean. We went to a Brazilian Steakhouse where they treated us like a couple with the waiter lighting candles and bringing us a bottle of champagne. We had a good time!"

"Oh, did y'all? He told us y'all just went to get something to eat, but he didn't say it was like that! Y'all were on a date?"

At that point, I didn't know if I had said too much, but I didn't think it was a big deal. I wanted them to know we had delicious food and the service was up to par. Of course, being around a bunch of men, their childish mindset led them to believe our time spent away from the group was a date. Furthermore, his downplaying what happened had everyone questioning if there was something extra going on between us. Did I think he was attractive? Of course, but I didn't think much of us spending time together because I knew he was with someone, and it was my wedding day. Plus, he didn't know I had previous relations with two of the groomsmen ten years prior. My goal was to get my mind off things. If I had to spend time with a guy for almost an entire day drinking, going to the ocean, and having a luxurious dinner, then so be it. After the guys finished teasing us about our day date, I hurried off to my room to get dressed for one of the most epic nights of my life.

The red dress I chose to wear that night was the same dress I wore in Vegas nine months prior when I was with my ex. I hadn't worn that dress since then, but my last night in Miami was not going to be defeated. I slipped on my six-inch heels while clutching my purse that had "Sex" written across it. I wanted to feel sexy. I wanted to feel wanted again. I put on my dark shades and went down to the groomsmen room. They were all dressed and ready to head out to have a night we would never forget. The hotel valet pulled the Tahoe truck around to the front of the building. We hopped in and were off to the strip club.

When we arrived at the club, there were hardly any cars in the parking lot. I was not sure how going to this strip club was going to go since they always made me feel uncomfortable. That night, I was no longer uncomfortable. I was ready for whatever was thrown my way. We walked to the entrance and waited outside for almost twenty minutes. More cars and other party groups began to arrive. Some groups were all women. After the best man spoke with the woman at the entrance, she motioned for us to enter the building.

I'd heard many things about this strip club. Many celebrities and rappers frequent it, and the women are some of the best strippers in the state, if not in the country. We picked our table, and we were immediately approached by half-naked, curvy, beautiful women. I was astonished at their aggressiveness and how fast they came over to us. Since they weren't paying me any attention, I went to the exchange desk to turn my twenty-dollar bills into one-dollar bills. I had never done anything like this before. I couldn't believe I was going to pay a stripper to either receive a lap dance for myself or one of the groomsmen. The most I had done at a strip club was sit in the corner where I was out of sight so I couldn't make eye contact. I always assumed that if I made eye contact with a stripper, they would think I was interested in women. I'm glad that night none of those assumptions got in the way of the best night of my life.

As I looked around the room, the strip club was as big as a warehouse. The poles appeared to be as long as a football field. They went from the top of the ceiling down almost to the floor. It was unbelievable. As I returned to our table, the DJ got on the mic and began playing music. The crowd was hyped up, and the strippers began performing. It truly was a work of art. Unbeknownst to me, the DJ was informed that our groom was getting married next week. He asked him to come to the stage. Of course, he raced to the stage, and we followed behind him.

The strippers on the stage pulled the groom up and started to dance on and around him. Since I had money, I began to throw my dollar bills. We all cheered him on. Of course, it was inevitable that the stripper who saw me throwing money on her and the groom decided to pull me on stage. She began to grind on my backside. I was a little embarrassed but went with it. I never liked going to strip clubs before, yet I always wanted to perform as a stripper as a bucket list wish. Here was my chance, and I looked like a timid mouse.

This woman had huge breasts and a big booty. I couldn't compare. She began to put her hand up my dress and feel on me. She whispered in my ear and told me to take off my dress. *"Bitch! Are you nuts?!"* She didn't know I had on Spanx, which had a few holes in them. My moment as a stripper was not going to end with me on stage in holey Spanx. So, unfortunately, I politely declined her request and hopped off stage. Part of me felt pissed I didn't have my moment as a stripper. Hopefully, I will get another chance.

As the groomsmen got off stage, the party walked back to our table. Because we reserved the table, it came with one bottle of alcohol. Sparklers attached to a bottle came floating through the crowd. A group of strippers delivered the bottle to our table. The DJ not only played a specific song when someone bought a bottle of alcohol, but the whole club made a big scene about it. I assumed this was a way for the strippers to know that table had money to spend. Well, I had money to spend that night. We popped open the bottle and began to pour drinks. When I took my first sip, I knew it would be the start of a night I didn't want to end.

As we began to throw back our shots and drinks, a bachelorette party was called to the stage. The next set of events blew our minds away. The DJ told the bride-to-be and her party to get on stage and begin dancing. Of course, she and her girls didn't hesitate. As they began dancing, the DJ started bribing them to take off pieces of clothing to earn what we thought was a free bottle of alcohol. Without hesitation, they began to take off their clothes one piece at a time. By the time the DJ offered four free bottles, every woman on the stage was naked - no bra, no underwear, nothing. It was a sight to see because they were not strippers. These were everyday women who didn't give a fuck about what anyone was going to say.

I instantly regretted not taking off my dress. They looked so carefree; they were having fun, and they weren't going to let anyone stop that, even if everyone in the building judged them. At the end of the song, the DJ told the naked women on stage he would offer them four free bottles of water. Because he never said specifically the type of free bottles he would offer, the entire building erupted in laughter. The women walked off the stage with their pride still intact. That was such a dick move but well worth the excitement.

The DJ introduced the next stripper that would be coming to the stage. She was skinny, which is not your typical build for a stripper. She had small boobs and a tiny shaped butt. He was hyping her up and encouraged everyone to run back to their seats to see her perform. I was thrown off by her appearance, so I was sure she would not do anything spectacular. I was wrong. The music started, and it was like living in stripper heaven. She began to do these acrobatic moves on the stage while spinning on the pole. It was something none of us had ever seen before. The stripper had the crowd so alive that we were all standing up on our table and seats cheering her on.

It was as loud as a sports arena in the building. It was insane. And, before I knew it, my first stack of one hundred ones was gone. I had no clue what I spent it on, but I knew I had to find an

ATM quick. I needed more drinks, the strippers were ready to get paid, and I was paying. As much as I didn't want to spend more money, my mentality was in "fuck it" mode. Everyone around me was having so much fun with no thoughts of their worries or troubles. I didn't want to worry about mine either.

Since we were out of alcohol, I purchased the next bottle. It was delivered like the first bottle of alcohol. There were sparklers, strippers, and the DJ shouting us out. All the strippers ran over to us and began dancing. The one stripper I saw had dark chocolate skin. She had weave down to her ass and reminded me of myself. Her skin was smooth. She appeared to stay longer at our table than the other strippers, so I welcomed her to stay with an incentive.

That incentive was a lap dance for the groom and myself. She appeared to be down to Earth and the best-looking woman in the building. I wanted to take her home. I had never felt attracted to a woman before and never thought I would pay to have a personal lap dance. Who was I? What was this? Am I into women now? I didn't know where this was going, but for the moment I wasn't going to stop it. Although, I would never interact with a woman sexually, admiring one with dark chocolate skin and a curvy body is always good for the soul. Apparently, all the groomsmen agreed, too.

Before the night ended, I paid for more lap dances and even gave some out personally. Letting loose was the top priority, and I planned to keep going until I couldn't go anymore. The night was young. I wanted to be young forever. As my eyes began to get low from all the alcohol and my speech was starting to slur, I was pulled aside by the best man. He told me words I needed to hear but didn't expect.

"Just so you know, the n**** who played you, ain't shit! Keep your head up! You know you deserve better, so don't sweat that!"

I knew I deserved better. I knew my ex played me. I was trying to keep my head up. My eyes began to fill with water, but I quickly blinked so the tears wouldn't fall. As much as I tried to pretend everything was okay, he must have sensed I was hurt. Although I was proud of myself for getting through the entire weekend without crying, it felt good to hear those words. It reassured me that it was okay to be mad, upset, and even angry. Getting married is a big deal. So, when the person you're supposed to marry drops the ball and leaves you hanging, it is devastating. I'm not sure how the best man knew I was trying my best to keep it together, but he did. I will be forever grateful for that moment.

As I sat waiting at our table for our last photo to be taken, the man I had spent all day with on the beach became extremely close. We danced together a few times, and it was refreshing, but I knew he had someone. The alcohol made him appear more attractive, and the attention he was giving me felt good. We walked to the car talking and slightly holding hands. Unfortunately, I was not paying attention and tripped and fell. The alcohol was in full effect. As I laid on the ground, my big hair seemed to be weighing me down. I couldn't get up or move. I wasn't offered any help getting up. Maybe he couldn't lift me because of his small build. I liked small men, but he was useless in this case. Fortunately, the other groomsmen were much bigger and carried me back to the truck.

During the ride back to the hotel, we stopped at a fast food restaurant and purchased food. I'm not sure if the cashier was annoyed with us, but her customer service skills were unprofessional. We made sure we told her about herself, too. Unfortunately, I was sitting all the way in the back of the truck. So, I couldn't throw my packet of sauce back in her face. After we pulled off, I sat back and began to enjoy my food. My crush sat next to me. He leaned over and whispered in my ear.

"You look so good tonight."

I smiled shyly and continued to eat my nuggets.

"No, for real! You look really good tonight!"

As I continued to smile and eat my food, I knew he was feeling me. He leaned in and kissed the corner of my mouth. I turned away quickly because I knew this couldn't go any further. I didn't have time for wrecking anybody's home, especially after mine got wrecked. It was hard. I wanted to keep the "no fucks given" mentality going, but it had to stop there. He lived two hours away from me and had a child. Plus, I saw the picture of the mother of his child, and she is much bigger than I am. I learned to pick my fights wisely, and I wanted no part of this fight. Regardless of what I wanted, I had to face the reality that being reckless was not the road I wanted to go down, especially with a guy who already had a family.

We arrived at the hotel. I hopped out the car and ran to my room. I thought I had to throw up, but I didn't. I jumped on the bed. I made it through the day. I made it through the night. My wedding day was over. I survived. I woke up to the sun glaring through the window. I laid there staring not wanting to go back home to reality. I wanted to stay there. It was like I had started a new life in the Sunshine State, and the only thing I wanted to see was the sun. I looked at my red dress that was thrown on the floor thinking it would be forever filled with chaotic memories - memories I never wanted to erase. Ironically, even when I wore it in Vegas with my ex, it was the first time I had been to Vegas. This dress will be the hall of famer of all my dresses.

I dreadfully put on my beach pants and tank top knowing my fun was ending. I went into the bathroom and collected my makeup and toiletries. I put all my barely folded clothes back into my suitcase and headed down to breakfast. The groomsmen were already there. They had two plates a piece. Greedy bastards. I sat my luggage down at a table across from the groomsmen and took my plate through the breakfast buffet line. I got scrambled eggs, bacon, a waffle, and strawberries. That's always been my favorite breakfast meal besides cereal.

While sitting around, I observed we all looked hungover. At first, there wasn't much talking. Then, one of the groomsmen started to talk about the strip club. Everyone at the table had a grin on their face, even me. We began to crack jokes about who got the most attention from the strippers and how amazing the performances were. I had never seen so many big asses and boobs all at the same time in my life. We loved every bit of it, and we all paid the price being dead broke the next morning. It was well worth every dime.

As we rode around South Beach one last time before heading to the airport to catch our flight, the guy I spent the day with at the beach became sick. He was drinking dark liquor the night before, and it didn't appear to sit well in his stomach after breakfast. I sat in front of him and could hear him moaning in the backseat. He was leaned over sweating profusely. I was scared he was going to vomit on my back, so we decided to turn onto a side street and jump out of the truck to let him vomit on the sidewalk. He was losing all his cool points with me. He couldn't hold his liquor nor pick me up after my fall last night in the strip club parking lot. I was over it.

All the groomsmen pulled out their phones and began recording him hurled over while his legs and arms were shaking. It was exceptionally funny to watch. The fast-food restaurant staff next door witnessed to our dramatic display of pettiness and began to laugh along with the people waiting in line to get their food. We hopped back in the truck and threw a bag back to Mr. Vomit. Then, we traveled back to the car rental place. Because of our run-in with the police two days before, I was livid. We explained to them what happened, and I demanded they give us the rental for free since they put stolen license plates on the rental truck. They continued to apologize for their mistake, but that wasn't good enough for me. I stormed out of the car rental place and snatched my bags to wait for transportation services to return us to the airport. This wasn't a battle I was going to win, and I knew if I ever returned, they would never get my business again.

Our bus arrived, and we were headed back to the airport. I was not in a talking mood because our money was not returned from the rental car place. So, the groom began to sing. Over the past twelve years I've known him, every time we would be on the phone, he would open the conversation with a song. It annoyed the shit out of me, but he did it anyway. On the way back to the airport, I wasn't having it.

As he began to sing, in a rage I shouted, "Shut the hell up!" Of course, he thought it was the funniest thing in the world, but I continued to face forward and not give in to his immaturity. Our driver unloaded our luggage out of the transportation van. Our flight was delayed another thirty minutes, but it was okay because we got to take one last airport selfie before heading home. The other female in the group pulled out a selfie stick and took our picture.

As soon as I saw the selfie stick, I immediately had a flashback. While lurking through my ex's page five months before, I discovered that the girlfriend's profile picture of her and my ex was taken with a selfie stick. I swore to myself I would never buy one because it would always be a reminder of my ex and the girl he cheated on me with. Nevertheless, I didn't want to let anyone know I was triggered, so I took the picture anyway. It was painful, but I did it.

It was our turn to board. I walked down the aisle looking for my seat. Once I found my seat that was next to the window, I closed my eyes. I knew the next time I would open them I would be back home. When we landed, it was dark outside. The only other female in the group offered to drive me home. Fortunately, she was one of my best friends as well, and the car ride on the way home further let me know why we were friends. As much as I didn't want to have the conversation, we did.

"Have you talked to him?"

"Hell no! I would never talk to that motherfucker again!"

"Did something happen again?"

Teary-eyed, I said, "Yes, the girl he is with tried to reach out to me."

"For real?! What she say!?"

"She wanted me to help her or some shit. I wasn't on it, but after she explained how he gets drunk and pick fights with her while she has a daughter and she's pregnant, I figured I might as well tell her. He's her headache now."

In utter shock, she asked, *"WOW! Would you ever get married again?"*

"Honestly, I can say right now. I would never do this again. He played the shit out of me in front of my friends and family. I was embarrassed. I was humiliated. I made the wrong decision. I didn't ask to be with him. He asked me. I feel stupid."

She warmly replied with tears in her eyes, *"I feel you girl. It's going to be okay. Everything is going to be okay."*

I was hoping she was right. The sixth man off the bench is supposed to save the team. Right now, I was the one who needed to be saved. I got back home and immediately started finalizing my book edits. My book was releasing in the next four days, and anxiety and excitement were taking over. I had spent the past eight months writing out my life from age five to twenty-eight. I took a publishing course, marketing classes, and even hired a program web designer. Since it was my first time selling a product, I had to start a business, which involved filling out paperwork and filing it with my home state to certify that I was a legit business. The process was tedious but worth it because I had learned something new and managed to follow through with my plan, even with a broken heart.

Becoming an author had always been a goal, and I was willing to do what it took to achieve it. I wasn't confident in my writing skills, and I knew my story would shock many people. I didn't have the white picket fence, two-parent family upbringing. All I knew was food stamps, electricity shutoff notices, and boys. It was not good, and no one knew about it - not even my closest friends. Shit, not even my mother. I hid my emotions, depression, and all my other vulnerabilities while growing up. However, I managed to keep a smile and extrovert personality. I should have been the kid who was a pregnant teen, college dropout, and heavily into drugs and alcohol. Fortunately, I wasn't. I was proud of that and wanted other women to know their past did not determine their future. I wanted to set an example. I wanted to be living proof that you can make it out of a dire situation that you had no intentions of being in.

Since social media was the place to sell any products your heart desired, my book was all over the internet and on as many free platforms as I could upload it. I didn't know if my online marketing plan would work, but I was taking a shot at everything. My mentors were bestselling authors, and I wanted to be at that level, too. I was on the radio, I was doing interviews, and I was traveling to various places to make sure my book was in anybody's hands who wanted it - both online and offline. The hustle was real. It felt surreal to see my name on a book. I envisioned my book would be on the shelves at household name stores. I pictured myself sitting on Oprah's or Steve Harvey's couch.

This book gave me a glimpse of what my future could look like, and I was determined to get there. The tireless nights I spent researching ways to market my book was endless. Eventually, I became obsessed with being an entrepreneur. I realized I wanted to be an author full-time. I loved my profession, but writing made me feel free. I felt like myself. I didn't have to pretend to be someone else. Not to mention, as an entrepreneur, I could make my hours, and I could be as creative as I wanted to be. My mindset shifted.

After marketing the book for twenty-four days straight, I got the news I had been awaiting. Although my book was not free, I released a free excerpt from my book for potential customers. I was advised by my mentors to take this approach if first-time authors wanted more exposure. Therefore, I followed this plan. Unfortunately, there was a technical glitch, and a woman emailed me saying she did not receive her free excerpt from my book. I quickly panicked and began scrambling around checking my website and social media pages where my book was displayed. Lastly, I had to check the hosting site where my book could be purchased. This site was notorious for selling books and other products and was quickly taking over the online world.

When I clicked on my book, the title of best-seller popped up on the screen. I was stunned and became short of breath. My heart started pounding, and my hands began to shake. My hard work had paid off. I was finally a best-selling author. I had never dreamt such a thing would happen to me. I had fought a long fight. It was the first good news I had received since my breakup. I needed this moment. It was like I was in a daze. I got up and immediately called one of my best friends. He didn't answer, so I left a voicemail. My voice was shaky. "OMG! You will never believe what just happened. My book just became a bestseller."

I clicked over and called my mom. She was still awake.

"Mom, guess what?"

"What?!"

"I'm a bestselling author!!!!"

"Oh, WOW! That's awesome!"

I sent out a text to my other friends. It was past midnight when I received my good news, so I didn't want to wake them with a phone call. I was happy. I was finally on my way up.
My book was all over social media gaining momentum among many women. My book was graphic, raw, and real. I wanted to put myself out there with no guard. You couldn't tell me anything. I was a published author. Being an author kept my mind off my heartbreak. I was

racking in extra cash and achieved one of the biggest tasks I never thought I would. I thought my nightmare was over. Unfortunately, it was far from being over.

Although I pride myself on being honest in my first book, I had haters and naysayers. All throughout my life, I wanted to please people. I put others' needs before my own and always wanted to fit in. I never questioned anyone's motives, and I knew that if I did everything the normal way, people would like me. Regrettably, some people decided they wanted nothing to do with me and took offense to my story. Those people were individuals I called my friends.

I didn't give a fuck about what a stranger had to say about my book because nothing mattered in the world more to me than my friendships. I would fight for them. I would give them money when they needed it. I would spend time with them. I would make sure I was there emotionally for them. I would be their shoulder when they needed to cry. I would die for them. I was the definition of what you call a ride-or-die friend. Nothing came before my friends. Nothing.

Because I was so caught up in the success of my book, I rarely noticed the non-support of my friends. It wasn't until it was brought to my attention that one sentence in the book made others feel uncomfortable. It wasn't a significant factor because the book was about my life; however, others did not feel the same when my book referenced their personal life. I couldn't grasp the concept that many years of building trust was crumbling right before my eyes over thirty words in a book.

I was devastated and hurt. I didn't want this to happen. I had been on a high for two weeks straight and was starting to fade back into the darkness slowly. I wasn't sure what hurt worse, the failed engagement or long-time friendships ending. Not only that, I started to realize a few of them were absent when my engagement ended. They just disappeared. I didn't know why. I didn't ask why either. I concluded that I knew my place, and it didn't involve being at the top of their priority list.

I will admit, I always wanted to look like the strong one in the group. I wanted to pretend nothing fazed me and that I was untouchable when it came to a man trying to hurt me. Maybe they thought I didn't need their help. I normally didn't, but this time I did. Bad. There was so much I wanted to tell them. I wanted to let them know I made a mistake, and I would never do it again. I wanted to let them know I couldn't bear to wake up some days because I was in that much misery. I wanted to let them know I needed them more than I had ever needed them in my life. I wanted them to help me confront my depression and hurt. I needed a girls' night like no other, but I wasn't going to get it. It was a hard reality. I couldn't imagine moving forward in life without my friends.

If someone had asked five years prior if I would stop being friends with people who've known me half my life, I would think that person was high on drugs. The memories were countless. The laughter was endless. Completing each other sentences was over. Our differences in personalities were beginning to catch up to us. We wanted to coexist in a world that was telling us we couldn't. I had the warning signs. Many would question my association with them, but I would shrug them off. Outsiders' opinions didn't matter when it came to the friendships I took to heart. However, every one of those doubtful questions came rushing back.

Were those outsiders right? No, they couldn't be. They only saw what they wanted to see. I knew my friends. I knew them well. Or did I? I was wrong. My blinders were on, and I wasn't letting anyone tell me differently. Because of my negligence, I got burned. Do I think it was intentional? Absolutely not. After heated verbal exchanges, I had to admit to myself and them that my book reference of their personal life was wrong. I shouldn't have ever mentioned or referenced anyone's personal life without their permission. I womaned-up about it. I had to because it was only right.

Those other friends who disappeared off the face of the Earth while I was going through my breakup sat lingering in my mind. Even though I admitted to my mistake, I still questioned why we were in this position. Were we really separating? Did they really think I would intentionally hurt them after everything we've been through over the years? I knew we all had other friends outside our core group, professional jobs, and we were involved in relationships, but none of that severed our bond. We've gone through hell and back together. This time, we stayed in hell.

When we went our separate ways, and we stayed that way. My attitude had drastically changed. My mind frame was different. I was losing everything that had meant the world to me, and I didn't know why. I became cold. I became distant. I realized my life was changing and everything was out of my control. The only thing I could hold on to was my published book and school. Those were the only two things I knew I had for sure.

To have comfort, I backtracked and began to see my old fling who had the kid. We had spent over a year in an off-and-on again friends-with-benefits situation. No matter what, he would come to see me or vice versa. The last time was different. He appeared to be less passionate about seeing me and left my apartment right after we had sex. It stung me. I had lost again.

I knew I was fragile from the breakup, and my friendships with my girlfriends were ending, but he was the last person I could seek comfort from, and even that failed. The next time he sent me a message, I didn't respond. I could not afford to have any shitty people in my life. The twilight zone was happening to me all over again, and I didn't know how to get myself out of it. I would cry off and on and constantly beat myself up about the decisions I made in choosing a life partner, who ultimately broke me. I was angry about the effort I put into friendships that deteriorated faster than I could blink an eye. I was so upset; I even tried on my wedding dress to ease my comfort. WHAT A MISTAKE! The last time I had tried it on was when I was getting fitted. I just sat on my couch with tears in my eyes. I wanted the torment to end, but I was in for another ride.

Section III:

"I Ain't Sorry."

-Beyoncé

Although my book had gained momentum in my personal life, it had gained even more momentum in my professional life. To some people, it amazed them that I could publish a book during my graduate program. Shit, it amazed me, too. I was quite proud of myself for completing this goal. However, some coworkers did not approve. As expected, all of them were women. Working for this employer as a social worker was my goal when I graduated with my undergraduate degree. I worked my ass off to ensure I met their hiring requirements, and I would continue to pursue an advanced degree to be promoted to a managerial position. I had it all planned, and all my ducks appeared to be in a row. I had managed to work in my position for a year and applied to my graduate program, using my employer as an internship.

After I received my acceptance letter, everything was in place. I was going to school for my master's and would have a paid internship. Not many students had the opportunity to get paid for their internship; however, I felt I was blessed to have that chance. I didn't apply for the company's fellowship program because I didn't want to commit to a company for an additional three years. A lot changes in a three-year period, and there was no guarantee that I would get a manager position since the competition was fierce. Seventy percent of the agency had their master's degree in either counseling or social work, and I needed to be a part of that group so I could keep my options open not only in that company but for other job prospects.

There were a few things I had to do to get into my graduate program. One of those things was to develop relationships with other individuals who had their master's degree. I didn't know many people the first year being employed there, but I felt my personality could win a few people over. Eventually, a few of my coworkers noticed my hard work and offered to write my letters of recommendations. One of those recommendations came from a male. He had an awesome personality and appeared to appreciate all the work I had been doing to help him and the staff he managed. Our friendship took off.

Although we began to enjoy talking about our families, other job perspectives, and school, others in the company saw us in a different light. He was married, and I was single, so the conversations and whispers began. What more could I expect from a ninety-five percent female populated company who had stories of marital affairs to tell every week? When I caught wind of speculation that he and I were more than just friends, I immediately ended our friendship. I stopped seeking professional advice. I rarely accepted any work requests unless authorized by a supervisor, and conversations consisted of only hi and goodbye. I didn't want my first year in the company to be shattered because of speculation and rumors.

Many people were unaware of the entirety of our situation, so I decided to put more details of it in my first book. I was mad as hell! A single woman and a married man can't have a conversation without having to deal with the insecurities of others? Bullshit! Well, that was the wrong move. When my book hit the bestsellers list, I was excited to share the news with my internship supervisor. She was a mother-type figure to me. I could share anything with her, and she always had my back. I felt she had a special connection to her black students. She asked if she could share the good news with the company; and, of course, I agreed. I knew my book would make a few people uncomfortable and uneasy, but I wasn't expecting the biggest backlash of my life.

Once people read my story, things quickly took a left turn that resulted in my being moved out of my position and forced into another position. The embarrassment was real. Everyone knew who I was in the company and they found out I got moved into a different position due to the vulgarity in my book. When they pulled me into the office the first time, I was upset. I was asked about the graphic details in my book, which consisted of describing sex scenes. They even asked if I had slept with the male coworker who wrote my letter of recommendation.

I was eight months from graduating, and I couldn't believe out of all the things I would be in trouble for, it was for something I didn't do. I was devastated that I had worked so hard to earn my position and they were taking it away because they wanted to look good to their sister company, or so I thought. Even after I told them why my book was written the way it was, they still moved me out of my position. Luckily, my wage did not change, and they let me remain employed to complete school and my internship.

I had speculation of who sent the rumor around about the vulgarity of my book. There were a lot of whispers in the cubicles and giggles when I would pass them in the halls. Many of them were married, but for whatever reason, they seemed concerned with which males I engaged in conversation with. It was like high school. I was the cute freshman who made the senior girls mad that the boys they wanted were giving me their attention. Although some pretended they were mature and was not involved in the drama, I knew better. I couldn't trust any of these bitches. Not one.

I knew many of them had it out for me when I first arrived at the company. It was their constant supervision over me like I was their teenage daughter. It was their constant lies they told the few coworkers I did trust, and their constant effort to see me fail, not only at my job but to make sure I would break at any moment right in front of them. No matter what, I didn't let them see me sweat. I knew my place, but they apparently didn't know theirs. I wish I would have stood my ground and said something to them, but I couldn't. I had one mission, and it was to graduate. I couldn't mess that up, no matter how much I wanted to take them out to the playground and show them the cute freshman wasn't scared to throw down.

After being removed from my position, I had reached my limits. I was embarrassed because my coworkers falsely accused me of having sex with a married man, and I noticed some of my female coworkers had become distant. Some deleted me from social media and barely made eye contact when speaking about work. They were no longer happy to see me. They believed a narrative that was false.

It was eye-opening and hurtful at the same time. I had begun to question everything about my book. I was beginning to think I made a mistake. I was in too deep, and my career was on the line. Everything I had built from my relationship and friendships to my career had all crashed and burned before my eyes. Right when I thought I was moving forward, something was always knocking me back down.

All I wanted to do was be myself and give young girls hope by showing them you can come from nothing, make many mistakes, and still come out on top if you work hard. I realized these work bitches, my ex, and my ex-girlfriends weren't trying to hear that. I wanted to go out to a field and scream at the top of my lungs. After that, I wanted to hide in a dark room and stay in there until I graduated. I felt gutted. I felt someone took a knife and stabbed me several times. At that point, I would have preferred that because at least with being stabbed could be quickly fixed with some stitches and bandages.

I was the most vulnerable I had ever been in my life. I was twenty-nine years old experiencing something I would rather have gone through when I was twenty. At least when you're twenty, you and others can brush off these types of issues with labeling you "young and naïve." Since I was twenty-nine and well into adulthood, many surely believed I should have made better decisions in choosing a significant other, friends, and the exposure of my business in a book. My internship supervisor brought my ballsy decision to my attention. Once she found out that I was moved out my current position, she asked me if I would go back and change what I wrote in the book.

Stern with tears in my eyes, I said, "No, I wouldn't."

Softly, she said, *"Even if it meant that it would clear up what you said in your book? Those extra thirty words could have prevented some of the confusion and speculation others may have."*

Aggressively, I replied, "No, I'm not apologizing nor will I change or add any additional words. It was my book. If people want to assume, then let them do that."

At that point, I was heated. People wanted me to fit into their comfortability box, and I refused to do so. They wanted to me to apologize for my past. They wanted me to apologize for being honest. They wanted to make me feel bad for writing my truth. I wasn't doing it, and I was tired of being shitted on by everyone I had given my all. I had given my all in my relationship, almost moving out of the state and being forced to have a child I didn't want. I had given all my time and energy to my friends who I fought for and would die for at the drop of a hat. Lastly, I had given my all to a company that I worked for by working extra hours and being an outstanding employee evidenced by earning employee awards. The book was the only good thing I had left, and I was going to hold on to it with the tightest grip I had. Furthermore, I was going to let those motherfuckers know I wasn't sorry.

Mission IV: Crystal Rock

I had been in my new position for two months, and I hated it. Although it was a lateral move where I had the same title and wage amount, the work was entirely different. I had to police families and their children. It was a heartbreaking job. I didn't feel like a social worker who was helping families reunify. I felt like a correctional officer who had to watch inmates in a prison cell. It was the worst job in the company, and those who were in that position were treated with disrespect by both the company and families. I felt my life had hit rock bottom. I dreaded coming to work every day. I had to see old coworkers who knew why I was removed from my last position. I also had to try to fit in with my new coworkers who also knew why I was removed. The adjustment had me depressed all over again, and I was back in my dark space. I needed a break. I needed answers to why this was happening to me.

My high school girlfriend's birthday was around the corner. She wanted to have this huge birthday dinner at a brewhouse in Cleveland, Ohio. I was stoked because my male best friend of ten years and I were invited. They were two of the four friends I had left, so spending time with them was highly cherished. We arrived at the brewhouse which was near Lake Erie. It was a beautiful day outside. It was the middle of January with no snow on the ground and a breeze that was far from chilling. It was like the first day of spring in the middle of January. It was odd but pleasant. When we arrived, her friends and family were all gathered at a long table. At least thirty people were in attendance, and we were all in good spirits to eat and drink beer. I wasn't a beer drinker, but at that moment in my life, a beer didn't sound bad. We sat and laughed. Once the dinner was over, we continued the celebration at a bar next door.

Before walking in, I noticed a sign outside of the bar that pointed up steps. The sign read: "Get your palm read for $59.00." I had never been to a psychic before. I was always taught the only psychic I ever needed was God. I still believed that, but I felt God wasn't speaking to me fast enough. I needed to know why my life was falling apart, and I needed to know now. I didn't think I could make it through another tragic event. I told my male best friend I would come over to the bar after I finished and tell him everything. I was so scared that I started to sweat.

At first, I thought coming up there was a stupid idea, and I almost turned around and walked out. However, the lady came around the corner right before I turned around to go back down the steps. When she came over to introduce herself, I observed that she was dressed like a gypsy. She was soft-spoken, and she wore glasses and dangling earrings. She was very colorful. She motioned for me to come inside. I looked around the room and noticed the sculptural artifacts. There was limited lighting, but the details of the room were visible. She motioned for me to have a seat at the table, and then she handed me a basket full of crystals. She asked me to choose one, and I immediately panicked. I was hoping whichever one I chose would give me the best results. I ended up choosing the clear crystal.

When she sat down across from me, she asked my name, and then put a card down along with the clear crystal I picked. What she said next, literally blew me off my chair. I did not know this woman, and she did not know me. The only thing we knew about each other was our names. She began to talk about me going through a tough time. She said it was as if I was constantly being attacked by something. I could not believe my ears. Before visiting the gypsy, I had spent months of hardly sleeping. It felt like my inner peace was disturbed, and it was showing physically. I would suddenly wake up in the middle of the night in tears and breathing heavily. It was something I couldn't escape, and it was by far the worst thing I had ever been through. I felt that I had all the signs of PTSD. The shit was real.

As a social worker, many of my clients would explain the symptoms of their mental health disorders, and I could hardly relate. That day had come to an end. As she continued to talk, she said, the words I didn't want to hear.

"I don't want to offend you, but it seems as though you've become a bitter woman."

I never wanted to hear those words uttered out of anyone's mouth. Ironically, the lady I'd only known for twenty minutes spoke those words in existence. Unfortunately, she was right. For the longest time, I told myself I would never marry anyone again. When I was ready to be in a relationship, I vowed to myself to keep my relationship private and only go public once we already tied the knot. I took extreme precautions, but with a relationship failure, as I had, most women would do the same. As my eyes began to water, she moved on to better news.

"I see the letter M. It's really big."

I never told her I was in school, so I assumed the M meant my master's degree. At the time, I was four months away from graduating. If all else failed, M could also mean money. I was betting she meant my master's, but a small portion of me wanted it to be money. The next letters she said were very interesting. She didn't know if the letters stood for a person's first or last name, but those letters would be important to me in the future. One letter stood out. She claimed the letter B was off in the distance. She didn't know what that letter stood for but kept repeating it was off in the distance.

Before I left, she advised me to fill up a cup of water and light a candle every day for seven days. She told me every time the cup of water would dissolve, fill it back up. I was skeptical because I didn't know if it was a satanic ritual or magical trick. Either way, I knew I wasn't going home to do that shit. My momma taught me better than that.

As I walked down the steps toward the exit, I noticed it was still breezy and sunny outside. I was hoping no one would see any dried-up tears on my face. I walked over to the bar next door to locate the birthday girl and my male best friend. They were outside on the restaurant patio smoking cigarettes and drinking beer. When I arrived, they asked me how it went. Because my male best friend knows me very well, he automatically assumed I was crying when the gypsy gave me my reading. Although I hated that he brought it to my attention that I was sensitive, he was right. I felt like someone had just given me the news I'd been hunting. I didn't imagine things. I was damaged and broken. Almost a year later, I wasn't healed yet. I didn't know what it was going to take. Lighting candles and filling cups with water was not going to do the trick. I needed a revolution to start.

***

The next month was my state exam to obtain my clinical license. It was a difficult test, and I needed something to take my mind off all the chaos that was happening over the year. Test-taking always has an effective way to keep me focused. If I wasn't studying, within seconds my mind would wander off to think about I did wrong in my relationship. How could friendships I put some much effort into just crumble to pieces, and what was I going to do now that my company had shamed me for something that wasn't true? I studied for two hours a night every night. I went to twenty-four-hour diners just to get out of the house so I could stay focused. Sometimes I would stay at the diner until three or four in the morning so that I could be so sleepy when I get home that I would be too tired to think. Then, I could fall right into a coma when I climbed into my recliner chair.

On the day of the exam, I went to the testing center. I was nervous because this was the first time I was taking a clinical exam, and I was unsure of the process. The instructor went over the rules and walked over to my station where there was a computer, erase board and headphones. I had four hours to take the exam. I could barely concentrate because the woman next to me had on fake nails, and I could hear her stroke the keyboard. It was annoying. I knew I wasn't going to be able to pass. I was irritated, and my focus was off. When I clicked my answer to the last question, the results showed that I failed. Although students can retake the clinical exam in three months, I felt defeated. My losing streak was on a roll. I asked myself, *when am I going to stop being powerless?*

Mission V: Formation

I didn't think I would see the light at the end of my tunnel. I had struggled all year wondering about my shouldas, couldas, wouldas, and I was stagnant. It was the worst time in my life in almost thirty years. Although I painted the picture like I was happy when I went to work and when I was with the few friends I had left, I was dead inside. I didn't want to do anything; I didn't want to be around anybody. Luckily, my friends didn't give up on me. They continued to keep me busy with movie dates, dinner, and an occasional night out for drinks. Some days, I wanted to start explaining my feelings of hurt, loneliness, and pain, but I was unable to translate them into words.

It was an indescribable feeling, until one day the words were explained perfectly. Those words were eloquently sung by the most controversial entertainer of all time. She breaks records with her music and entertains like no other artist seen before. She was my idol. I respected her as a wife, mother, artist, and most importantly, a powerful woman. I had always wanted to be her growing up and would die at any opportunity to meet her. At the time, she wore gold-colored hair. She was the epitome of a black goddess. I loved her like she was my mother.

She released her most controversial song to date called *Formation* back in February of that year. Of course, many who did not understand what her song represented to the African American community caused a national debate, questioning her blackness and loyalty to mainstream music. That hit home for me in many ways. I knew about the struggle of pleasing the majority in the workforce by removing my cultural identity, and then finally being fed up by saying "fuck it" and wearing my big natural hair, while being proud of my big lips and negro nose. This song represented true blackness in its rawest form.

She did not hide who she was. She was not scared to speak politics. She did not once back down to the criticism. She stood her ground and asked for black women to join with her. Was she talking to me? She didn't understand that her song couldn't have come at a better time in my life. I had to stand with her. She was black like me. She had recognized society issues that affected our community, and she made sure her voice was heard at the biggest event in America. I was in awe of her brilliance and her ability to not give a fuck. I needed that motivation. I needed that attitude. Just when I was starting to give up, she came and swooped in like a crowned eagle ready to attack her prey, and she gave a glimpse of hope that everything was going to be okay after all.

Two months after being scolded for her blackness, she released her full black female empowerment album, and it was the right dose of medication I had been longing for all year. It only took a week for me to know all the words of each song. The words resonated with me so much that I had physical reactions to each song by either crying, yelling out "Yes, Lord," dancing, or clinching my fist because I knew motherfuckers were trying to play me and keep me down. That ended now. I sang those songs every day until I was no longer upset. I didn't know if this artist went through heartache, but it appeared that whatever hurt her, cut her deep. At that point, I didn't want to listen to any other artist or music. She and I shared something in common, and she was the only one who got me. We were determined to bounce back.

I watched her epic video with her twirling around in her gold dress swinging her bat while smashing car windows. That's what I wanted to do - go around smashing windows because I was so angry and filled with rage. I wanted to go on a rampage and slap anybody who looked like my ex. It almost happened when I went to school one weekend. I was walking down the hall to my class and glanced through one of the windows of one of the neighboring classrooms. I saw the back of a bald head and physically got ill. My heart started beating fast. If I had a bat, I would have walked into that classroom and bashed his head open until I could see the brain. I couldn't believe how angry and out of character I was. Now, I know how married couples end up on *Snapped*.

Since I couldn't bash his head in, I knew this rage could only be eradicated by smashing out windows and fighting those who put me in this mental war. Legally, that would be frowned upon in my profession; however, the mental battle was ongoing, and I was at my breaking point. I knew this artist and her music were my only saving grace. It's scary to think what would have happened if that album was never released. Suicide? At one point, I wanted to do it. I even admitted it to my college professor after I requested to step out of the room while he played audiotapes of military men calling the crisis line. They were giving up. They were tired of fighting. I was tired of fighting.

I could have quit my job, stopped attending school, and become a bum because I had lost all hope. I may have just isolated myself due to the embarrassment and humiliation I put my family through. I went to counseling, talked to close friends, and even entertained a psychic to get away from the shitty life I was having, but I felt nothing was working. I was wrong though. I was alive. I was still going to work, and I was a student. And, of all things, who would have thought twelve songs sung by a powerful black woman would be the icing on the cake to help me come out on top? The battle was over.

I was slowly winning my sanity back. I could feel myself starting to heal. I was starting to see the light. I wasn't hiding anymore. I was starting to smile again. I even thought I could give dating another try. I couldn't believe one careless decision turned my life upside down. But, after a year of pain, I was alive to tell the story and all the things I learned during my battle. I was ready to move forward. It was time to rebuild my life. I wanted to be confident again. I wanted to trust again. I wanted to be happy again. I wanted to be fierce again. I wanted to feel powerful again.

Section IV:

"Power is not to be given. It is to be taken."

-The
Mummy

Guide for Turning Sadness into Strength

Heartbreak is Powerful

Throughout this book, I spoke about how painful heartbreak is and how it affected my life negatively. One thing I can appreciate about heartbreak is that it was powerful enough to change me in ways I didn't imagine. For instance, it made me think. Yes, we think daily when performing ordinary tasks associated with our careers and education. However, we must think more when it comes to our personal lives, especially when it comes to relationships. Sometimes we get blind-sided by the glitz and glams, and we are not consciously aware of what could go wrong.

This is not to be negative but to encourage women to become aware of who they let in their lives. I knew damn well the dude I was with had red flags, but I ignored them, which resulted in my suffering from the most painful thing I've ever had to endure my entire life. I never thought of my plan if something went wrong. I never anticipated the wedding to be called off, nor what I would do if the guy I was with was a massive manipulator and liar. These are things I didn't prepare for, and I wasn't thinking about if they would cause havoc in my life. This is not to categorize all men as liars or cheaters. Instead, it's to help others appreciate that heartbreak is sometimes a blessing in disguise to better equip you for your next relationship.

Another way I realized heartbreak was powerful was because it brought out the resilience I didn't know I had. The saying, "You never know how strong you are until you have to be," was so true in my case. There were many moments I didn't think I was going to make it, but I kept pushing forward. I honestly couldn't tell you where the push was coming from, but I wasn't going down without a fight. I was searching desperately to find the light at the end of the tunnel. Luckily, I did. Sometimes when I hear about others who have gone through a comparable situation, I instantly think of how hard the struggle was and hope they see the light, too.

One person who began to see their light was an iconic singer who was the new and improved version of Madonna. She recently came out with her documentary, *Five Foot Two*, and it was a glimpse into her life as an artist and a woman. I had always admired her "I don't give a fuck" personality, too. She's a firecracker, and I am here for it. She wore the most outrageous clothes and hairstyles and pushed the cultural boundaries to the point everyone felt uncomfortable. Not to mention, her music has resonated with many people, including the LGBT community. She has saved many lives, and ironically, she and my favorite female artist have collaborated on songs and call themselves friends.

In her documentary, she discussed her engagement and how it was called off. She was humiliated and experienced loneliness due to her career sabotaging her relationships. I was wondering how could someone so powerful who's viewed as a role model for many young people be lonely? I realized it doesn't matter how much money and fame you have. When heartbreak hits, it is bound to change your life. There was sadness in her eyes when describing her engagement failing. I, too, had the same sadness. I realized she was no different from me. We both had suffered significantly.

In contrast, her heartbreak was amplified because her relationship was displayed on a public platform. Still, she kept pushing forward. I admired her resiliency as well. She didn't want to give up the fight. She wanted to overcome, and she did. I looked at her and realized I wasn't in this alone. Many women are going through heartbreak, and only we understand how painful it can be. I felt a newfound connection with this artist. Her song, *Million Reasons,* is one of my favorites. However, her documentary not only gave me a million more reasons to admire her as an artist, but I began to admire her as a powerful woman who turned her sadness into strength.

Surround Yourself with People Who Want to See You Win

One of the hardest things I had to learn was that not everyone who you surround yourself with wants to see you win. This is a hard pill to swallow. I know because I had to swallow this same pill. It's very simple; yet, most will not agree because of comfortability. Let's back up. It is important to understand that you know the people you surround yourself with every day. These people will be your foundation by default, and you must make sure your foundation is solid. If it's not, there is a possibility you will find a crack in your foundation and fall right through it.

I almost fell into that crack in both my personal and professional life. I had to realize that the same people who smiled in my face didn't want me to surpass them nor did they want to see me do well. I was utterly shocked and even cried because I thought I was well-liked among those who I had been around for years. Instead, these same people tore me down every chance they got, and they immediately turned their backs on me at the first sign of turmoil. Most of it was done behind my back, but once the betrayal came to light, I viewed people differently. I realized people were jumping off the ship quickly, and there was nothing I could do but stand by and let it happen while I was left to pick up the pieces.

Taking a hard look at the ones who came to my rescue while I was suffering from a failed engagement, criticism of my book, and the loss of my position at work, verified who was in my corner for the long hall. It was refreshing, yet hurtful. I felt like I had to start my life over beginning with new friends who believed in what I was doing with my life. Many people were satisfied with living to achieve the American dream of growing up, going to college, finding a well-paying job, and starting a family. That is how life was presumed to end for many Americans. Nevertheless, that was not my American Dream, and many people were uncomfortable with that, including the person I was going to marry. He didn't even want me to finish school. He wanted me to be (in his words) "barefoot and pregnant," which I was not willing to do. This is not the 1940s, and it was far from achieving the American dream I began trying to run after right after high school.

I wanted to be a writer. I wanted to own a business. Forget this working for the man bullshit. I wanted to be my own boss, and I was going to achieve that at any cost - even if that meant losing friends and even my job. I knew I was taking an elevated risk, and unbeknownst to me, not everyone was on board with that idea. At first, I thought I had made the wrong decision and would transform into a turtle by hiding in a shell to avoid the backlash. However, I realized if I was going to go down, I was going do it while doing what I felt in my heart was right.

I was going to follow my purpose. Those who wanted to support me on this journey would show up, and those who didn't would reveal themselves in due time. Although it was painful at the time, I look back and realize the abandonment from friends, coworkers, and my ex was for the better. As I continued my journey, I realized it was what I needed to reveal those who truly wanted to see me win.

Don't Give Up

The people you love will hurt you. The life you planned will not go accordingly. Don't worry because there will always be another door that will open. The pain won't last forever, so don't give up. There were many times I wanted to throw in the towel, and I had every right to do so. Everything was falling apart from my relationship to my friends and career within six months. I didn't know how much more I was able to take. Giving up seemed like the only option at various moments because the humiliation and embarrassment were eating me alive.

Don't let the pain eat away at you to the point you have nothing left of yourself. I had deep thoughts of giving up on life, and it was scary.

To some people, from the outside, I appeared to have it all together. They couldn't tell that I was hurt and didn't know I wanted to give up. Life was tough as shit! Still, I kept going. Instead of focusing on all the things going wrong, I had to change my mindset and focus on what I had going for myself and who I had in my corner. I had to realize that if I gave up, I would lose the little bit of myself and the hard work I put into school and finding my purpose. It wasn't worth it.

Part of not giving up is to stop making yourself continue to pay for your mistakes. Yes, we all make mistakes whether it's with the toxic partners we choose to date, jobs we choose to stay employed at after we know they've done us wrong, or the unsupportive friends we choose to keep in our lives. We've all been there. However, you must stay focused on what your end goals are, which may require self-evaluation.

Evaluating who and what you allow into your life is a part of not giving up. Making better choices is a part of not giving up. Moving forward is a part of not giving up. Wanting to have a better life is also a part of not giving up. I heard the phrase on a radio station once that said, *"Every setback is a setup for a comeback."* I believe this to be very true. No, you won't immediately see the light at the end of the tunnel because you will be blind-sided by other things. Yes, you will think your life is almost over. Yes, this heartbreak will send you to a place you've never been. I know because I was there. Just don't give up. Hold on like fake eyelashes in a windy storm. Hold on like your life is depending on it. In fact, your life *is* depending on it. Everything rides on your ability not to give up. So, don't do it.

Life and People Change Without Warning

If there's one thing I took away from my heartbreak, it's that life and people change without warning. Throughout life, we are taught to plan our next move. We do so out of habit. This is a very hard concept to break. Each one of us is taught to have a life plan. Unfortunately, many of us are not prepared when that life plan does not go accordingly. I was that woman, and you may be that woman, too. Here's the thing. I never planned to get married, step away from long-time friendships, or leave the employer I thought I would retire.

As for friendships, you never envision your life without certain people. When that moment comes where they will no longer be in your immediate circle, life gets interesting. The support system you built for twenty years evaporates in a blink of an eye. One day you're friends, and the next day you're not. As far as careers go, these days millennials are instructed to work jobs for two to three years and then move on. Old-school employees were raised to stay at a job for forty years and retire, and they would encourage young people like myself to do the same. Although that was the plan at first, it became a distant memory once I realized I had to move on. No job is worth staying at if you're punished for being misunderstood.

Change is difficult. It was hard for me to understand I was that girl who wasn't getting married anymore. After adjusting my life to make room for someone else, within twenty-four hours, I had to adjust back to being single. It was weird because I had been single technically for almost thirty years, so why was this so hard? It was hard because I didn't plan on being single once I was engaged. No one ever plans that! That was one of the hardest pills I had to swallow. The adjustment was grim.

When it came to my friends, it was almost like experiencing death. I wanted things to work out. I wanted things to go back to the way they used to be. I missed staying up late cracking jokes, spending countless nights each week at the bar dancing to the latest music, and figuring out what guys would be our potential Mr. Unfortunately, within a matter of weeks, I realized things changed, and we were headed in different directions, almost becoming complete strangers. I was never prepared for my friendships to wither away, but it was happening, and there was nothing I could do about it.

We all know choosing a company to retire from is important to set up our future. I had mine picked, but they didn't pick me. Although I was never forced out of the company, I was made aware I could never be in a managerial position. So instead of kissing ass, I hurried up and got my state license and master's degree and moved on. My services and time were no longer needed, and I realized I was not going to waste time with anyone who didn't value me.

Don't let Others Control Your Destiny

Going to college, buying a car, and obtaining full-time employment is what's considered normal in our society. Normal is not bad. Thinking others who don't follow the path of normalcy are abnormal is bad. However, you must not let others make you feel that they should approve your path to your destiny. I was a stickler for that. I always wanted approval from people. I don't know where I acquired such thought process, but it was ingrained in me up until I had no other choice but to choose a different path. For so long, I never realized I was letting others decide for me. I was letting the man I was in a relationship with push marriage and children onto me when I wasn't ready, and I was letting my job bully me into silence and make me feel insane for wanting to write a book.

When people don't approve of your lifestyle and decisions that would further make you a better person, they knock you back down to their level of normalcy. I was not going to let that happen, and you shouldn't either. If you don't want to do something that does not make you better as a person, then don't do it. There is power in the word NO, and I had to learn to start using it.

No, I wasn't letting another man coerce me into anything. No, I wasn't going to let my friends make me feel bad for telling my story. No, I wasn't going to let my previous employer make me feel like becoming a published author was a sin. I wasn't having it anymore. I had to make the decision that others were not going to control my destiny anymore, and anyone who thought they could kindly exit my life.

There may be some who may find this approach as uninviting or negative. However, there's nothing more important to protect than yourself. This does not mean step on or belittle people to move up. It means it's time to reevaluate your priorities. Always look out for yourself. Always put yourself first. Don't put others in the driver seat of your life because they may lead you to a place that may be unsatisfying.

Follow the 1% Rule

You will feel like you are going nowhere after experiencing a heartbreak. The days will get longer, and the darkness will be invading. You will feel like you are in quicksand sinking deeper and deeper every day. You will be so focused on the negative that you will miss the opportunity to celebrate your progress. Every day will be a struggle; however, it's important to give credit where credit is due. That credit belongs to you in every attempt you make to get up each morning to go to work, to hang out with friends, to start a new project, and anything that moves you toward healing your heart. That is what Author James Altucher describes as the 1% rule.

To break it down, James explains in his blog that the 1% rule is associated with dieting. He explains people who want to lose weight immediately stop eating all "bad" food. According to James, this strategy is ineffective due to people skipping the small steps to get to their ultimate goal of being at their desired weight. This same concept applies to heartbreak. You must celebrate the small steps to get to the bigger goal. And, that goal should be to heal.

A little effort every day is the 1% you celebrate. You can't just jump in and think you will be able to cut off your feelings and hurt, and then hit your goal by the end of the week, end of the month, or even the end of the year. You must take note of your small steps to appreciate your progress. It was hard for me to appreciate the strength I displayed every day by still going to school, publishing my first book, and even managing to celebrate my wedding day in another state on a beach.

I felt negativity was all around, and I couldn't escape it. However, I didn't realize the 1% I demonstrated every day to move toward healing my heart. Was it tough? Sure. But, when I look back, I missed out on appreciating the progress I was making. Don't miss out on your 1%. Give yourself credit. Count the small steps.

Section V:

"If at first you don't succeed,
dust yourself off and try again."

-Aaliyah

The Triple "P" Plan

If you follow me on social media, you may have seen that I released a quick easy-read plan for women who've gone through a breakup and struggled to move forward. Although the guide can help you push forward through your hard moments, adding this plan will give you another boost to understanding your feelings and moving forward with life after a devastating moment. I created The Triple "P" Plan after my horrible heartbreak. I had never been hurt like that in my life. It took a year and some change to get back to my normal self.

Honey, let me tell you… The road was not easy. Women go through heartbreaks all the time. I couldn't relate at first because I was never in their shoes - at least not to that magnitude. However, things quickly changed. Having your heart broken is a life-changing event for sure. Women either grow bitter or better from it. Most women I was surrounded by or saw on TV were very bitter. I didn't want to be that woman.

Who does the "Triple P" Plan help? What is it anyway? The "Triple P" Plan was created to solely help women who have been broken by the man of their dreams. We, as women, cut ourselves down in relationships because we are nurturers by nature. Therefore, we tend to put others first before ourselves. We tend to give our all while in relationships, and we are willing to go through a lot to keep the person we are dating or married to in our lives. So, let's get into the plan and put a rest to that madness.

You must go through the PAIN.

Per Oxford's Dictionary, *pain* is defined as a "range of unpleasant bodily sensations produced by illness, accident, mental suffering or distress." (Oxford, 2009, pg. 593) One of the hardest things you must do after getting your heart broken is to go through the pain. There is no way to go around it. I've tried multiple attempts at coming up with solutions on how to skip past this fucked up stage, but I came up short-handed. At first, you may be in shock, so the pain may not hit you right away. But, when it does, hold on for your dear life! It's like you're on the rollercoaster from hell! Your mind is racing a mile a minute, and you don't know whether to scream, cry, throat-punch a stranger, kill your high school bully that you see living they're happily ever after all over social media, or just disappear off the face of the Earth.

You're going to want to call up a few of your besties and "blow down on this fool" or "turn up" on his ass. Shit, you may even want to call his momma and cuss her ass out too for raising such a poor excuse for a man. There's a lot of things you're going to want to do and say, and guess what? It's perfectly okay. (Well, not the killing part because that's illegal, but everything else stands.) The pain will sometimes become unbearable like causing headaches, sickness, or loss of appetite. You will be triggered by everything that reminds you of him. His cologne, the car he drives, the sound of his name, the favorite places you went as a couple, the gifts he bought you, pictures you took, the sex, the moments you spent with each other's families will all trigger painful memories. If he has children, you will be reminded of the moments you shared with them, too.

Each time one of these things shows up in your presence, your heart will beat fast, your mood will change, and you will get sick to your stomach. It won't be fun for you at all. The worst part about this is that you never know when it will end. It's an ongoing fight with your heart and mind. So, unfortunately, I hate to be the bearer of bad news, but there's no time-limit on healing the heart. You will hurt, it will be painful, and it will feel like it's going on forever. However, you must keep moving forward the best way you can, and the "Triple P" plan will help you along the way.

Most importantly, while you're going through all these pains, find someone to support you. Experiencing the pain of a broken heart is hard enough, but to go through it alone is what I call "rock bottom." It is a dark place, and I wouldn't wish it on my worst enemy. So, I encourage you to confide in someone you trust and discuss the pain you're feeling. This person could be a close friend, a mentor, a pastor, a professional, a co-worker you can trust, your family, hell, even the mailman if you trust him.

The point is, get your frustration and pain out to someone who cares about you! Don't go through this alone. You're going to feel embarrassed, sad, and even upset at yourself because you're in this situation because of a dickhead you thought was Prince Charming. Trust me, girl, I understand. This is all a part of the process. You might feel as though you have gone mad. And, maybe you did for a little bit. It feels like you're losing the fight, but rest assured, you got this! To continue to move forward from the pain, you've got to figure out what's next and that's to…

Find your PURPOSE in life.

Normally, this would be established first, but some start later in life, and that's okay. For me, while I was in engaged, I was writing my first book. Something about being a writer and putting my story out to the world about the difficulties of growing up without a father made me feel like I had a purpose in life. I felt there were plenty of women across the world who could benefit from my story, and I wanted to help as many as I could. It fulfilled me in ways a man couldn't. Still, to this day, I believe it's one of the best decisions I've made thus far. Now, most of you may not want to be writers, and that's fine. I'm sure there's something you've always been passionate about and wanted to pursue.

This doesn't necessarily mean go out and start a business - by all means, do so if you want. It just means, do what use to make you happy or will make you happy. For me, it was writing. For you it may be scrapbooking, traveling, cooking, making new recipes, stand-up comedy, dancing, healthy eating, starting a charity, volunteering, spending more time with friends and family, exercising, reading, starting a new home décor project, going back to school, etc. Whatever it was you desired at one point, go back and do it! When you find your purpose, it will almost feel like you've found freedom. What I mean by freedom is, you will find something that helps you become more of yourself. It's like when you find what you want to do or enjoy doing, it feels like a missing puzzle piece that finally completes your whole picture. That's how writing was for me, and I hope while reading the "Triple P" plan, you can find the puzzle piece you've been missing this whole time.

Another important factor when it comes to finding your purpose in life is that people may not always agree with or support you. And, you know what?! That's okay, too. It isn't their life! If you're taking the opportunity to do what makes you happy, and it doesn't affect you or anyone else in a negative way, then tell those bitches to move to the side. I know it sounds harsh, but some people have a hard time watching others do what they've always wanted to do and being happy for them.

Jealousy is an ugly trait. Someone who has always wanted to be free and happy within themselves but can't because they "settled," can't stand to see you thrive. Honey! Honey! Honey! The hate and jealousy become real. Hence, why I mentioned to only confide in those who you know have your best interest. It is real out here in these streets!

Make no mistakes, finding your purpose while healing from a breakup gives you clarity. You get to see a whole new you. You gain so much more insight, wisdom, and preparation for your next step. You may not see it at first, but the small steps you take count towards moving forward. Just like the step you took today by reading the "Triple P" plan... You are ready for a change. You are ready to heal and find your purpose. Once you go through the pain and find your purpose, there is one final step in your plan. And that's to...

Wait for the next PENIS to find you.

Yes, you read that correctly! The word *penis* is there. And, guess what, there will be another penis... I mean, man that comes along in your life! Why? How? Well, because this plan isn't to help you grow bitter; it's to help you grow better! I know you didn't think you could just move on with such great purpose and no pain and not expect another man to join the party, did you? News flash, there's always going to be a man coming your way, but this time, you are much more prepared. Now, you know how the old saying goes, "To get over a man, you have to get (under) a new one." This isn't entirely false. Ok, let me be serious for a moment…

Most women do this every time they go through a breakup, and there's nothing wrong with it. However, where it becomes a problem is when most women who aren't over the last man end up dumping all their extra baggage into the new relationship and expecting the new guy to play Captain-Save-A-***. The point of this plan is to help you become successful at dating, making sure that when the next penis comes your way, you will be able to figure out his "fuckboy" tendencies early on before becoming heavily invested. This is something I've gotten good at since my break up, and it has saved me a lot of tears. For that, I'm thankful. Don't worry; you will get better at it, too. All it takes is some time and a little bit of clarity, and you got this!

Now, if you go back and read the first word of the sentence again, *wait,* that's exactly what I meant. As women, we tend to rush into dating someone or putting all our eggs in one basket because we want marriage and children before our biological clock expires. But, I say WAIT! STOP! HOLD UP! I get that it's the 21st century and women are more aggressive, but I promise you can't keep a man unless he wants to be kept. You can have all the clarity you want in the world and even be at the top of your game with education, health, and looks. Still, if he isn't ready, you will be in the same situation you were before. And, of course, I don't want that for you.

When a new penis comes your way, that means he is interested and possibly waiting to see if it can grow into something more. Luckily for you, you are already ahead of the game because you've been through the painful stage. Therefore, you aren't looking to be saved. You found a purpose which has given you freedom and clarity on what you want out of life, and now you're just waiting for someone to complement that.

If for whatever reason, the penis interested in you doesn't fit into your puzzle, it will not be the end of the world for you. You won't go back to that dark place that you were in before. You may still call up your homegirl and tell her the dude was a joke, but it won't be a two-hour all-out crying session. You'll simply move on and keep being yourself while enjoying your freedom until someone worth your time comes along.

Before going any further, just know… The Triple P Plan takes hard work. This isn't going to be a walk in the park. This is how life goes - not just with relationships, but with friends, family, and jobs as well. You will be hurt many times and fall several times. But, none of that matters. All that matters is how you get up and move forward. I am living proof that I counted myself out of the game and didn't think I would survive when I went through my breakup. However, the Triple P Plan helped me get back on my feet and not count on anyone to save me. I had to bounce back and save myself. So, this year, make sure you are not waiting around for another Prince Charming to save you from your last heartbreak. Bounce back, save yourself, and turn your sadness into strength.

About the Author

Ikeshia Capre has been a blogger since 2013. She prides herself on keeping it real on paper. She is the author of the Amazon #1 Bestseller *Dear Dad, I Broke the Cycle: A Grown Woman's Guide to Getting Over an Absentee Father*, which was released in October 2015. It is now available on Amazon. Ikeshia's book, *The Year of the Woman: A Guide for Turning Sadness into Strength* is a continuation of her story. It reveals what led to her failed engagement, loss of friendships, and changes in her career. Ikeshia graduated with her bachelor's degree from Kent State University and her master's degree from Case Western Reserve University. Currently, she is a doctoral student in Clinical Psychology. Ikeshia serves as a Medical Social Worker in Ohio, her home state.

www.ingramcontent.com/pod-product-compliance
Lightning Source LLC
Chambersburg PA
CBHW060505030426
42337CB00015B/1748